THE CRY OF MY HEART

TIM HAWKINS

HOW TO BE A GENUINE DISCIPLE

THE CRY OF MY HEART

The cry to be real – the cry to be genuine –
how can you stand strong in a world that is fake?
Come and have your life turned upside down by
Jesus' teaching in **'The Sermon on the Mount'**.

LEARN HOW TO BE A GENUINE DISCIPLE

BY TIM HAWKINS

I want to include everyone!

I want everyone to feel that they are included in this book. This can be a little difficult with the limitations of the English language. Historically, the male pronouns 'he, 'his', 'him', (and their derivations) have been used to include people of both genders. However, not everyone feels included these days by following this tradition. I have avoided the perfectly correct, but cumbersome alternative of always delineating 'he/she', 'him/her' etc. To try and include everyone, I have opted for the grammatically incorrect, but inclusive 'they', 'their', 'them' etc. I hope that you feel included, and that you do not cringe too much with the damage I have done to the English language! – **Tim**

The Cry of my Heart
First published in 2006 by Tim Hawkins
This UK edition © Tim Hawkins/The Good Book Company 2008

The Good Book Company
Elm House, 37 Elm Road
New Malden, Surrey KT3 3HB, UK
Tel: 0845-225 0880
E-mail: admin@thegoodbook.co.uk
Website: www.thegoodbook.co.uk

Hawkins Ministry Resources
42 York Road, Kellyville. N.S.W. 2155 Australia
Tel: (+61 2) 9629 6595; Fax: (+61 2) 9629 6595
E-mail: info@hawkinsministry.com
Website: www.hawkinsministry.com

ISBN 13: 9781905564781

Artwork by ninefootone
Printed in the UK

CONTENTS

The Cry of my Heart encouraged me to stand up for Jesus and to put my neck on the line, like he first did for me.

Craig, Year 12

1 DIDN'T YOU KNOW THERE WERE RULES?

Don't you just love it when you're absolutely succeeding at life? When you're cruising in top gear; nailing your studies; sinking the shots; kicking the goals; attracting the girls (or guys) and everyone looks at you and says:
'I want what you're having!' 'I wanna be like you!'

All of us want to feel like we're achieving some sort of success. That life is worth living. That we're getting on top. That there's nobody who can bring us down.

1. THERE ARE RULES TO FOLLOW

And you've probably worked out by now there are rules you've got to follow if you want to come out on top. I don't mean official written-down rules. But in every area of your life there are **unwritten** rules – guidelines that you're expected to live up to... and there's no way you're going to be a success if you don't understand and follow these unofficial regulations.

As a little kid, someone made up a rule that you weren't allowed to step on the cracks when you walked along the footpath...

Somewhere in primary school, you discovered that on your birthday, some kids had a rule that they had to punch you – one punch for every year of your age... *(ouch!)*

In secondary school, someone made up a rule that the back seat on the bus was the place of honour, and only incredibly cool kids were allowed to sit there ...

School for me was a tough time. At my catholic boys-only college there were all sorts of rumours about... well... you know... catholic boys at catholic boys' schools, where we were taught by unmarried men who all wore glasses and long black dresses! As students, we were very determined to show that we were real blokey-blokes – and we all knew that there was no way in the world that you would ever be accepted or envied or admired if you broke any of the unofficial 'rules' in how to be a blokey-bloke.

If you wanted to succeed at my school, you had to understand that there were a whole lot of unwritten rules you had to follow, so you could avoid ever being thought of as 'sexually suspect.' It didn't take much to have someone call you by a very unflattering nickname. Here were the things to avoid to make sure that no one would call you 'gay'.

a) Never wear shorts to school

Shorts were one of the options for our summer school uniform, but no one at my school was game to wear shorts – because as soon as you did, you would be labelled 'gay'. Even on the hottest summer day, we sweltered away in our long trousers. Better to be unbearably hot than to be thought of as 'uncool'.

b) Never wear white socks

For some reason, white socks were deemed to be 'uncool'. I don't know why – but they were, and everyone knew it. No one would be caught dead in a pair of white socks. It was a sure sign that you were weird.

c) Never carry an umbrella

Umbrellas are incredibly sensible things to carry when it is raining. But not at our school! Umbrellas were a certain give-away that you were definitely sexually-suspect. Better to be covered in rain than to be covered in shame!

d) Never drink strawberry milk

It was probably the pink colour that doomed this particular product at our school canteen. No self-respecting boy would buy it. Drinking strawberry milk was decidedly uncool. In the end our school canteen had to stop stocking it. They couldn't even give it away!

e) Never pull the bus cord

This one actually caused the most problems. Fortunately, this did not occur at my school, but at another boys' school down the road. They had decided that pulling the bus cord (to tell the driver to stop at the next bus-stop) was the wettest thing ever. The result? Boys went kilometres out of their way – not being game to pull the cord – and desperately hoping that some other poor kid would pull it for them and suffer the indignity of having the whole bus look at them with fingers pointing and yelling insults! Not very smart, but I guess it kept us fit.

You see, if you want to be a success in life, you've got to know the game plan. You've got to know the strategy so you can win the fight.

Still not convinced there are unwritten 'rules' for success? Well, think about

'IF YOU WANT TO SUCCEED, YOU HAVE TO KNOW THE GAME PLAN'

the unwritten 'rules' that exist for getting to know guys and girls.

2. RULES FOR UNDERSTANDING WOMEN

Can I just talk to the guys for a moment? *(Girls, you can skip to the next heading if you like).* Guys – you know that if you ever want to be a success with girls, you've got to understand the rules they live by – and the rules they have for us. Girls will always say that these rules are not true. **But fellas – you all know – if you don't understand these rules, you don't get anywhere.**

I'm not sure I actually believe all these rules. They certainly don't apply to everyone. But see what you think!

a) Women never have anything to wear. You might see a wardrobe full of hundreds of different outfits, but men, you just don't understand. She has nothing to wear.

b) A man can take 5 minutes to get ready for the big date, but women need a lot longer. Learn to be patient!

c) All women believe they are overweight, **but you must never agree with them!**

d) Women do not want an honest answer to the question: 'How do I look?'

e) It's okay for girls to go to the toilet in pairs, or in small groups. It's kind of a social excursion. **Guys must NEVER do this!**

3. RULES FOR UNDERSTANDING MEN

Girls, you know if you want to be successful with guys, there are rules you've got to understand. Ignore these rules at your own peril!

a) Guys never need help. They might be completely lost – in a strange part of town, with no idea how to get to their destination – but they **never need help**. You need to understand that reaching for a street directory, or *(heaven forbid!)* actually asking someone for directions, would be a denial of their basic manhood. And they **certainly** don't need help from you *(even if you're right – which you probably are!)*. Work out what you really want – do you want to get to your destination, or do you want to keep your man?

b) Being faster/better/stronger/cleverer **really** matters to them. Don't ever suggest that you know a better way. Don't ever beat them – at Trivial Pursuit, at arm wrestling, at **anything!** Their fragile masculinity probably can't cope with it.

c) They have selective sight and selective hearing. They can spot a new-model car half a kilometre away, or notice a new hamburger joint under construction, but don't expect them to notice that you've had your hair cut or that you're wearing a new outfit. When they're watching the footy on TV, they will listen intently to every word of the commentator, but they may not remember anything personal or precious you have said to them. If you ever hear the phrase *'yes, dear'*, you know they haven't heard a word you've said.

d) Strong emotions are reserved for sport, cars and gadgets. Apart from these three items, there is no discernable difference between your man when he is angry, your man when he is sad, or your man when he is asleep. One mood fits all.

e) When a man does a minor chore around the house – like emptying the dishwasher – he will act like he's just cleaned the whole house and deserves a few hours off as a reward. Just smile... and sigh.

I don't know whether any of these rules are true or not, but certainly guys and girls are different. If you don't know the rules *(and who really does?)* – if no one ever explains them to you – it will be very hard to be successful at your relationships.

4. WOULDN'T IT BE GOOD IF SOMEONE EXPLAINED THE RULES?

Wouldn't it be good if someone sat down with you and explained all the rules – and mapped out an entire strategy for you – so you could be successful with **the opposite sex?**

Wouldn't it be good if someone sat down with you and explained all the rules – and mapped out an entire strategy for you – so you could be successful with **your life?**

C'mon! You want to be successful in what you do! But you need someone who understands it all to sit down and explain the whole thing to you.

Sometimes that's exactly what happens.

> You're in the army – and your battalion has to go and capture a village so you can free the innocent people who have been held hostage. The night before it all happens, your commanding officer stands in front of your troop and says: *'Here's the battle plan. Here's how we're going to win. Here's how every one of you can be successful.'*

'WOULDN'T IT BE GOOD IF SOMEONE SAT DOWN WITH YOU AND EXPLAINED ALL THE RULES?'

> Or maybe you're on a sports team – and your coach sits down with you on the sideline before the match, and says: *'Here's the game plan. Here's how we're going to win. Here's how every one of you can be successful.'*

Wouldn't it be great if this could happen in your everyday life? Wouldn't it be great if this could happen in your Christian life?

Wouldn't it be fantastic if Jesus could sit down with you and look at your life – and look at your relationships – and how things are at home – and at church – and at school – and look at your future – and your struggles – and your obedience – and your ministry and your opportunities – and Jesus would look you in the eyes and say to you: *'Here's the game plan for your life. Here's how you're going to win. Here's how you can be my faithful disciple on this crazy planet. Here's how you can be effective at winning your friends to also be my disciples. I have made you and designed you to be a success on this planet. Here's how to do it.'*

Wouldn't that be the coolest thing possible? If Jesus could sit down with you and say: *'Here's how you can be a success at being my disciple. Here's how you can be a success at changing this world for me.'*

5. THAT'S WHAT THIS BOOK IS ALL ABOUT

Everybody wants to be genuine. Everybody wants to be real. That's the cry of **everybody's** heart. We're going to look at three chapters in the Bible where Jesus sits down with his disciples and explains how to be genuine. Jesus is going to explain to you all the rules – he's going to show you all the guidelines – he's going to give you the battle plan – to show you how to win – so that you can be his genuine disciple.

Genuine in the way you remain faithful to him. Genuine in the way that God uses you to change the lives of those around you.

Jesus doesn't want you to be a half-hearted disciple – or a 'when I feel like it' follower – or a 'one day when' believer – or a 'maybe tomorrow' Christian!

Jesus doesn't want you to be a half-hearted, wishy-washy, namby-pamby, mealy-mouthed, lazy-dog, uncommitted, wake-up-at-midday, never-say-a word-about-your-faith, sit-on-your-backside, don't-give-a-stuff disciple who is totally indistinguishable from all the unbelievers who live on this planet.

Jesus has called you to be different. Jesus has called you to be genuine. Jesus has called you to have a future that is genuine, a ministry that is genuine, an impact on this world that is genuine. Jesus has called you to have a life that is genuine.

He has placed you on this planet so that you will be a genuine disciple for him. As you read this book, imagine that Jesus is going to sit down with you and explain to you the game plan – explain to you how to live for him and achieve the things that he has destined for you.

Are you ready? Let's start by looking at what it means to experience **genuine success!**

2 A WHOLE NEW WAY TO SUCCEED

Matthew 5:1-2

We're going to turn to Matthew chapters 5 to 7 and see how Jesus teaches us about genuine success. Let's set the scene:

Jesus has just called his very first disciples. They've heard him teaching the crowds. They've seen him healing the sick. They've watched him casting out demons.

There are large crowds being attracted to Jesus. But Jesus wants to take his troops aside. He wants to sit down like a coach before a footy game – and show his disciples the game plan for how to live their life. The crowds are half-listening in the background. But what Jesus really wants to do is instruct his troops on how to be genuine disciples.

> **'JESUS WANTS TO GIVE YOU THE GAME PLAN FOR YOUR LIFE'**

Matthew 5:1-2
'Now when Jesus saw the crowds, he went up on a mountainside and sat down. His disciples came to him, and he began to teach them, saying ...'

Right now Jesus wants to instruct you. He wants to give you your game plan for your life. He wants to show you the way to live so that you will have genuine success.

In fact, he wants to turn your idea of success upside down. Jesus is going to make eight statements about the person who is truly successful. Eight descriptions of the sort of person he wants you to be. See if you can take each of these eight pictures and make every single one of them the cry of your heart.

1. WHAT'S THE DEAL WITH BEING 'BLESSED'?

If you look ahead at Matthew chapter 5, you'll see that verses 3-11 all start with the words *'Blessed are ...'*

5:3	*'Blessed are the poor in spirit...'*
5:4	*'Blessed are those who mourn...'*
5:5	*'Blessed are the meek...'*
5:6	*'Blessed are those who hunger and thirst for righteousness...'*
5:7	*'Blessed are the merciful...'*
5:8	*'Blessed are the pure in heart...'*
5:9	*'Blessed are the peacemakers...'*
5:10-11	*'Blessed are those who are persecuted...*
	Blessed are you when people insult you...'

Do you kinda get the feeling that Jesus wants us to know what being 'blessed' looks like?

So... what **does** it mean to be 'blessed'?

'Blessed' is a difficult word to translate precisely. Other Bible versions use words like 'happy', 'lucky', and 'spiritually prosperous'. But they don't quite convey the full meaning either.

The person who is blessed is the person to be envied – cos they've got what God wants them to have. The person who is blessed is the person that we shout *'Congratulations!'* to. The person who is blessed is the person who is achieving real success – a person to be admired, a person to be honoured, a person that you would really want to be like.

If someone was truly 'blessed', you could walk up to them, slap them on the back and shout: *'You're the man! You're the bomb! You're the one we all want to be like!'*

Jesus is about to describe the sort of person who has made it. He wants to show us how to have genuine success. And maybe, as he goes through this list, he will turn your view of success upside down!

If you asked your friends to describe someone who was successful – I wonder what words they would come up with? *'Rich... strong... happy... powerful... has the best of everything... lots of friends... climbed over everyone else to get to the top of the tree... great personality... popular...'* And I guess the list could go on.

The message from Jesus in Matthew 5 is *'Your view of success might not be big enough'*. It's almost like Jesus is saying *'I want to give you a bigger view of success'*. You can imagine Jesus challenging us at every point and declaring *'I want to change forever the way you look at success'*.

2. RE-DEFINING SUCCESS

I'm going to suggest a definition of success for you. See if it works for you:

**'Success means feeling good
because you're achieving something good'**

Let's have a closer look at that:

a) Feeling good

You might be a successful business person, a champion sportsperson, or a top notch muso; you could be Mr or Miss Popular at your school, coming first in your exams, making lots of money... or whatever; you might achieve everything possible in your world – **but still not feel good about it!** Imagine achieving something great – but not feeling satisfied! Imagine being on top – and still feeling empty! Imagine accumulating all the goodies you can possibly dream of – and not enjoying any sense of satisfaction or pleasure at all!

But there are stacks of people like that. Top musicians – top sports champions – multi-millionaires – people who have all the rewards of success, but who live very unfulfilled and unhappy lives.

Success is not worth achieving unless you feel good about it.

b) Achieving something good

To be successful doesn't just mean completing what you set out to achieve. What you achieve has to be something worthwhile. Something beneficial. Something really worth achieving. Something good.

If you don't achieve something which is 'good', then you end up with a very warped view of being successful. If you take this crucial factor out of the equation, then you could conclude that the most successful man of 2001 was Osama Bin Laden. He executed his plan to near perfection – he brought down the World

Trade Centre in New York – killed thousands of innocent people – brought mass panic to the USA – and took the battle against terrorism to an entirely new level.

But you have to ask – is what he achieved really worth it? Was it beneficial? Was it 'good'? Is Osama Bin Laden the person you want to look at and say: '*He's so successful – I want to be like him*'? I don't think so!

If '*achieving something good*' isn't part of your equation, then you could conclude that the most successful leader of the 20th century was Adolf Hitler. He had a vision – he had a plan – he executed it masterfully. But look at the result. Six million Jews exterminated. Many more innocent people imprisoned, tortured and uprooted from their homeland. Half of Europe invaded and occupied, and a World War lasting over 6 years.

The things he achieved – were they good things? The things he achieved – were they things that were worth achieving? Can you look at Adolf Hitler and say with admiration: '*I want to be just like him!*'? I don't think so!

Compare that with another well-known person of the 20th century – Mother Theresa of Calcutta. A picture of success? She was born poor – and died poor. She had none of the trappings that we normally associate with success. She dedicated her entire life to caring for the poverty-stricken, starving, HIV-infected peasants in the cultural backwaters of India.

But check back to our definition of success – '*Feeling good because you're achieving something good*'. Is Mother Theresa a picture of success? Is she someone you can look at and say: '*I want to be like her*'? Absolutely!

'CAN YOU WORK OUR WHAT THE 'CRY OF YOUR HEART' REALLY IS?'

What she achieved is real success – '*Feeling good because you're achieving something good*'. Wouldn't it be great for you to achieve that too? Wouldn't it be great if you could feel good because you know you're achieving something good? Wouldn't it be fantastic if you could feel satisfied because you're achieving the things that are actually worth achieving?

Let's look at Jesus' eight pictures of the person who is blessed – his eight definitions of success. See if you can work out what 'the cry of your heart' really is. Let's be prepared to have our whole thinking about success turned upside down.

3 A DISCIPLE LONGS FOR WHAT IS RIGHT

Matthew 5:3-6

Jesus is about to give us eight pictures of what it really means to be a genuine disciple. Eight definitions that will turn our understanding of success on its head. Eight descriptions of the person who really is to be congratulated. Eight images of what it means to be 'really cool'.

Here are the first four. They all describe the genuine disciple who is longing for what is right. Check out each one: *'Is this really the cry of my heart?'*

PICTURE 1 – POOR IN SPIRIT

Matthew 5:3
'Blessed are the poor in spirit, for theirs is the kingdom of heaven.'

Probably the first word we would think of to describe someone who is successful is the word *'rich'*. And yet the first word that Jesus uses to describe someone who is successful is the word *'poor'*. Jesus describes people who are *'poor in spirit'* – that is, people who know that they are *spiritually poor*.

ARE YOU SPIRITUALLY POOR?

Spiritually poor? This simply means people who know they can't make it to God by themselves. Jesus' first picture of success is someone who knows they really need God.

Jesus tells a story about two blokes. *(You can look this story up for yourself in Luke 18: 9-14.)* Anyway – these two blokes both decide to go into a church to pray. The first one is a bit of a low-life – from the criminal end of town. Never done anything good in his life. Never been to church

21

in his life. Probably never prayed before. He knew he had nothing to bring to God. He knew he didn't even deserve to be there. So he stayed down the back of the church, knelt down, kept his head bowed low, and prayed: *'God have mercy on me, because I am a sinful man.'*

The second bloke also walked into the same church to pray. This man was a good man. One of the best. A holy and righteous person. A leader in his church. He felt confident before God – and walked right up to the front of the church and prayed boldly in a loud and triumphant voice: *'God, I praise you that you have made me good. Thank you that I am honest. Thank you that I give so much to the poor. Thank you that I attend church once each day and twice on Sundays. And thank you that you have made me to be so much better than that miserable man cowering down the back.'*

Jesus makes this point about that story; only one of those two men did the right thing that day. And it wasn't the man who **looked** and **acted** successful. It was the man who came before God honestly, and knew that deep down in his heart he desperately needed God. That was the cry of his heart.

Sometimes we can be tempted to think that we're the hottest stud-muffin that God's ever had on his squad. Sometimes it can be easy to think that Jesus is kinda lucky that we've decided to sign up on his team. But the truth of the matter is simple: when we come to God, there is nothing that we can bring with us – and we desperately need his help.

Does that describe you? Is that the cry of your heart? Do you really know that you need God? Is your life totally dependent on him? Are you truly spiritually poor? Are you genuinely *poor in spirit?*

If that describes you – then Jesus says: *'Congratulations! You are the one who is truly blessed. You are the one who is to be envied above all. You are successful because you will receive the one thing that is really worth having. **The kingdom of heaven belongs to you!'**

PICTURE 2 – THOSE WHO MOURN

Matthew 5:4
'Blessed are those who mourn, for they will be comforted.'

Once again, one of the key words we would think of to describe someone who is successful is the word *'happy'*. And yet Jesus now describes the person who is successful as being someone who *'mourns'*.

This doesn't just mean being upset because something rotten has happened to you. It's really got to do with being upset by the same things that upset God. Jesus is talking about a person who is upset by the sin that they see.

How do you feel when you see the sin that is in the world? Does it get to you when you see people taking advantage of others? How do you feel about the sin in your own life? Does it matter to you that you do stuff that is wrong?

Is that the cry of your heart – *'I'm upset by the sin I see'*? When you see the stuff-ups that you make and the sin that sits there in your life ... are you saddened by that? Does that weigh you down?

Are you like that? Is that the cry of your heart? Does sin really upset you? If that describes you – then Jesus says: *'Congratulations! You are the one who is truly blessed. You are the one who is to be envied above all. You are successful because you will receive the one thing that you really need. **You will be comforted!**'*

PICTURE 3 – THE MEEK

Matthew 5:5
'Blessed are the meek, for they will inherit the earth.

'Meek' is one of those words that doesn't get much of a run these days. No one ever wants to admit to being *meek*. It's probably used as a bit of an insult. Someone who's a bit weak. Someone who's a bit wishy-washy. Someone who's a few kangaroos short in the top paddock. Unfortunately it rhymes with *weak*, *geek* and *freak*.

But there is a real strength in the word *meek*. Meek does not equal weak. Meek does not equal wimp. Being meek means keeping your **strength under control.**

That's the way Jesus is described.

Matthew 21:5

'... See, your king comes to you, **gentle** and riding on a donkey, on a colt, the foal of a donkey.'

That word *gentle*, which is used to portray Jesus, is exactly the same word as the word *meek* that Jesus uses to describe the truly successful person. And that description of Jesus – on the donkey – is talking about the day when he would ride in as king to the city of Jerusalem – and be hailed by the admiring crowds. Certainly not a picture of **weakness.** *Meekness* means *strength under control.*

'BEING MEEK MEANS KEEPING YOUR STRENGTH UNDER CONTROL'

Imagine a huge articulated lorry – the biggest truck you can get. Deep-throated pistons of throbbing horsepower. A mighty truck. A powerful truck. Enough grunt to run you off the road and smash you into gravel-sized particles. And yet this powerful truck is purring motionless at the traffic lights. Stopped because of one red light. Amazing strength – but kept under control.

That's *meek.* **Strength under control.**

Does that describe you? Amazing strength kept under control? Are you a person who doesn't try and force their own way? Are you willing to tame your strength and give up your rights so you can be gentle and caring with others? Are you okay if you stop trying to force your own ideas and your own way even though you know you could? Is that the cry of your heart?

Do you have that humility? Are you willing to give up anything? Because Jesus says: 'If you're willing to give up anything – you will gain everything!'

Read again what Jesus says in Matthew 5:5

'Blessed are the meek, for they will inherit the earth.'

No wonder Jesus describes meek people as successful! **Look at what they will inherit!** Not just a small reward. Not just a free set of steak knives. Not just a new mobile phone when you sign up for a 2-year contract.

No! You inherit the whole entire earth!

Meek. That is Jesus' picture of success. Does that describe you? That you use your strength – under control – in a gentle way? That you're willing to give up everything... and you don't try and force your own way?

Are you like that? Is that the cry of your heart? Well, Jesus says: '*Congratulations. You are a success in God's eyes! You will inherit the new creation God is making!*'

PICTURE 4 – HUNGER & THIRST FOR RIGHTEOUSNESS

Matthew 5:6
'*Blessed are those who hunger and thirst for righteousness, for they will be filled.*'

Jesus is describing people who really want to see this world run his way. People who are just longing for the day when Jesus will return and put an end to this mess.

When you look around your home, do you hunger and thirst to see it run God's way? When you look around your school, do you long to see it turned upside down for Jesus? When you look at your own life, do you just ache to see the way you live turned around by God's Holy Spirit?

Is that the cry of your heart? '*I really want things done God's way!*'

We're not talking about a person who just shrugs their shoulders and says: '*I wish things could be better*'. We're talking about someone who is hungering and thirsting for righteousness. To see things work out **right!**

Notice that Jesus talks about people who are **hungry and thirsty** for righteousness. He is talking about people who have a **deep inward longing** for things to be done God's way. He's talking about **hungering and thirsting** for righteousness. Not just **snacking** on righteousness.

Christians sometimes just 'snack' on righteousness. They have just a *little bit* of righteousness – just enough to look good as a Christian – but have never taken Jesus seriously. Come on! Jesus wants you to hunger and thirst for righteousness. Not just to have a spiritual munchie at the righteousness snack-shack.

As a Christian, are you ever tempted to be content to have spiritual junk food?

God's righteousness is not meant to be a little snack that gives you a quick spiritual fix – something that makes you feel good now, but nothing really changes about you. If you are truly hungry and thirsty for something – you'll do almost **anything** to make it happen.

Are you absolutely hungering and thirsting to see God's righteousness unleashed in your world... in your school... in your relationships... in your personal life?

ARE YOU CONTENT TO HAVE SPIRITUAL JUNK FOOD?

Does that describe you? Is that the cry of your heart?

Then Jesus says:

'*Congratulations! You are the one who is truly blessed. You are the one who is to be envied above all. You are successful because the one thing you are really hoping for – it will happen! You will be satisfied! You will be filled!*'

4 A DISCIPLE STANDS FOR WHAT IS RIGHT

Matthew 5:7-12

Jesus now gives us four more pictures of success. These all describe someone who stands up for what is right.

PICTURE 5 – THE MERCIFUL

Matthew 5:7
'Blessed are the merciful, for they will be shown mercy.'

Merciful. You show someone mercy. You help someone when they don't deserve it. You're not looking to pay back even when they are wrong. The person who does **that** is a success in God's eyes.

Oh – it's easy to only help the people who **do** deserve it. We can be so nice to the people who are nice to us. There is always a temptation to only give things to people who have earned it.

That's not the way Jesus wants you to be. He wants you to be merciful. **Because that's the way he treats you**. He had mercy on us when we did not deserve it. He died for us while we were still sinners. He even reached out with forgiveness to those who were driving the nails into his hands.

Is that the way you want to treat others? Do you truly want to treat people the same way Jesus has treated you? Is that the cry of your heart?

Does that describe you? Is that the cry of your heart? Then Jesus says: *'Congratulations! You are the one who is truly blessed. You are the person who God loves to show mercy to!'*

PICTURE 6 – THE PURE IN HEART

Matthew 5:8

'Blessed are the pure in heart, for they will see God'.

Jesus is describing someone whose heart is absolutely sincere in following Jesus. He is describing someone who isn't pretending with God. He is describing the person who doesn't only act like a Christian when they're around their Christian friends, and then dishonour God with their life when they're away at home or at school. Jesus is after people who don't pretend with him – people who don't try and hide things from him.

'IF YOU'RE NOT HIDING FROM GOD – THEN GOD WILL NOT HIDE FROM YOU'

Is that you? Is that the cry of your heart? Can you wholeheartedly say: *'I'm not pretending to be Christian!'*?

If you're not hiding from God at all – congratulations. You are a success! And guess why? If you're not hiding from God – **then God will not hide from you.** The promise of Jesus in verse 8 is sure and certain to those who are pure in heart – **you will see God.**

PICTURE 7 – THE PEACEMAKERS

Matthew 5:9

'Blessed are the peacemakers, for they will be called sons of God.'

Jesus is describing someone who is totally at peace with God. Someone who is totally forgiven by Jesus. Someone who is a close friend of God – where there is no barrier between the two of you.

And when you have experienced that true peace from God, you will want to live in that same sort of peace with all the other people around you.

You will live at peace with your family.

You will live at peace with your friends.

You will even live at peace with your enemies.

Does that describe you? Think about your situation at home. Are you a *peace-*

maker? Do you help bring peace to the relationships at home? Or do you tend to incite World War III? Think about this: do you think that things are more peaceful at home **when you are there;** or do you have the sneaking suspicion that things are actually more peaceful at home **when you're away from your family?** *(If you're feeling really game, ask your mum!)*

Jesus says: *'Blessed are the peacemakers'.* Does that describe you? Is that the cry of your heart – *'I want to forgive and accept others'*?

If you are bringing the peace of God to the relationships around you – then Jesus says: *'Congratulations! You are the one who is truly blessed. You are the one who is to be envied above all. You are successful because you are God's child.'*

PICTURE 8 – PERSECUTED FOR RIGHTEOUSNESS

Matthew 5:10
'Blessed are those who are persecuted because of righteousness, for theirs is the kingdom of heaven.'

Let's imagine that you're being a genuine disciple the way that Jesus wants you to be. Think back over the pictures of success that Jesus has been painting for us.

Admitting that you're spiritually poor...
Grieving over your sin...
Meek – with your strength under gentle control...
Hungering and thirsting for righteousness...
Merciful...
Pure in heart...
Bringing God's peace...

That isn't going to exactly bring you into the cool crowd at school is it? That's not going to necessarily make you Mr or Miss Popular. That's not going to get you free membership of the 'it crowd'.

In fact – you might get picked on. People might make fun of you. You might run the risk of being *'persecuted because of righteousness'.*

This persecution can take many forms:

> You desperately want to invite your friends to your youth group or Church... and every time you ask them, they laugh at you – and look at you with that *'Why would I?'* look – and you think: *'They'll never come'*.

> You stand up for Jesus at a Christian event at your school – and your so-called friends laugh at you.

> You let your friends at school know that sexually you are keeping yourself for your future marriage partner – and they think there's something wrong with you.

> You won't join in something wrong that your friends are doing, and they call you *'that goody-two-shoes'*. And you find that you're not invited to the next party that your friends organise.

Persecution can come from your enemies. But the cruellest persecution comes from your friends. You can be persecuted at a state school. You can be persecuted at a church school. You can even be persecuted by your family.

Jesus says: *'If you're going to stand up for me, you've got to risk being rejected by the cool crowd.'*

Matthew 5:11
'Blessed are you when people insult you, persecute you and falsely say all kinds of evil against you because of me.'

Has that ever happened to you? How did you feel?

Matthew 5:12
'Rejoice and be glad, because great is your reward in heaven, for in the same way they persecuted the prophets who were before you.'

If you're going to put Jesus' radical teaching into action in your life, you've gotta risk being rejected by the cool crowd. You've gotta risk being persecuted!

Why?

Because they persecuted Jesus! And if you're going to be like Jesus – at some stage you're going to be persecuted too!

John 15:20
Jesus said: 'If they persecuted me, they will persecute you also...'

Jesus got strung up on a cross because he stood up for God's righteousness. If you're going to make a stand for Jesus – then you need to realise that the same thing might well happen to you.

Is that the cry of your heart? Can you honestly cry out: *'For the sake of Jesus ... I am prepared to risk being rejected by the 'cool' crowd!'?*

If that describes you, then Jesus says: *'Congratulations!'*

Matthew 5:10
'Blessed are those who are persecuted because of righteousness, for theirs is the kingdom of heaven.'

Jesus says: *'If you're being persecuted because you're a member of God's kingdom – congratulations... because you **ARE** a member of God's kingdom!'*

PICTURE 9 – HOW YOU'RE GOING NOW

'Picture 9? I thought there were only 8 pictures!'

You're right – Jesus gives us eight pictures of success, but they are of no importance without Picture Nine. Because without Picture Nine, these previous eight pictures can be just theoretical. Jesus wants **you** to be a success – and so **Picture Nine is a picture of you**. So – how are you going at being the successful person that Jesus wants you to be?

Do you remember our definition of success?

'Feeling good because you're achieving something good'

So, check it out. What are you achieving? What are you spending your time and effort on in your life? What makes you feel good because you're getting on top of it? And here's the important question – **Is it something that is really worth achieving?**

Wouldn't it be a terrible shame to get to the end of your life, and look back at all the things you had achieved, and to work out that none of it was really worth achieving?

Wouldn't it be a waste to end up spending all your time doing stuff that really didn't matter?

So – what **is** really worth achieving? Simple! Becoming the person that God has designed you to be! Is that something that you're game to put all your heart and soul into?

'But how do I do that?'

'ARE YOU ACHIEVING WHAT IS REALLY WORTH ACHIEVING?'

That's what the rest of this book is about. That's the master plan that Jesus has for us. That's the coach's instructions for the game of life that Jesus teaches us in Matthew Chapters 5 to 7. That's what we're going to learn as Jesus trains us to become **genuine disciples.**

5 A DISCIPLE MAKES A DIFFERENCE
Matthew 5:13

1. NOBODY WANTS TO BE IGNORED

I don't think I've ever met anyone who **likes** to be ignored. All of us like to think that people are taking notice of us. All of us like to think that we can make some sort of a difference. It's great when people love us; it's survivable when people hate us; but it feels **absolutely awful** when people ignore us!

Do you ever feel as if no one really takes any notice of you? It's a horrible feeling! So I got to thinking – I wonder who are the **most ignored** people on this planet? Here are my top three:

a) Cabin crew

You know, those neatly-uniformed staff members who stand up in your aircraft on the runway and give you the safety demonstration.

Have you flown recently? Have you noticed what happens during the safety demonstration? Here is a dedicated professional attempting to give you the information that you need in an emergency. Here is a well trained and highly-skilled employee who is showing you crucial techniques that may save your life. And guess what? **Everyone on the plane is ignoring them!** Casual flyers are gawking out the window; business flyers are sipping their pre-flight drinks; frequent flyers have their heads buried in newspapers; and nervous flyers are exploring the delights of the airline's sick bags. **No one is listening!**

b) TV Wrestling Umpires

Now, think about any sport. The job of the referee or umpire is to control the sport. Make sure there is a fair outcome. Make sure that the players don't break the rules.

Imagine this scene on a TV wrestling show: 'Killer Krebosky' has 'The

Slab' lying on the canvas *(I'm sorry – all wrestlers have weird names)*. 'Killer' is about to reach for a folding chair conveniently located just outside the ring. He is planning to wreak havoc on the unprotected head of his opponent. This is **way** outside the rules!

The referee moves in. He argues with 'Killer' for a moment, and directs him to put the chair down. He waves his arms vigorously to indicate that what 'Killer' is about to do is a bad, bad thing. What happens? **The referee is totally ignored!** 'Killer' assaults 'The Slab' with the aforementioned chair; does serious damage to both the chair and his opponent's head, **and then has his arms held high by the referee as the winner of the match!**

c)   Teenagers and children in shops

You know the drill. You're standing at the counter. A number of adult customers have come up to the counter after you. **You're** meant to the be the first one served. The shop assistant comes over and – guess what – **all the adults get served first!** Even though your money is as good as everyone else's – somehow you get left till last.

Don't you hate it when you're ignored like that? You're trying to have your say – and no one listens. You ask someone to do something – and they just don't do it. People walk past you as if you don't even exist.

2. WE ALL WANT TO MAKE A DIFFERENCE

I suspect that all of us want to be able to make some difference in the world. All of us want to be able to have some impact on the people we meet. At the end of our lives, I'm sure all of us would like to look back and think that we had contributed something significant to the running of this planet.

Jesus wants his disciples to make a difference. Jesus wants his followers to have an impact. Jesus doesn't want you to spend your days following

an insignificant belief and drifting invisibly through a world that never even notices you. When you're living as a genuine **disciple**, Jesus wants you to have a genuine **impact**.

This has got nothing to do with your personality. You can have an outgoing, vibrant, bubbly and strong personality. Or you can be a quiet, shy, individual sort of person. It's not your **personality** that will make an impact on this world – it's your **lifestyle**.

Remember the lifestyle that Jesus has already outlined?

5:3   *the poor in spirit...*
5:4   *those who mourn...*
5:5   *the meek...*
5:6   *those who hunger and thirst for righteousness...*
5:7   *the merciful...*
5:8   *the pure in heart...*
5:9   *the peacemakers...*
5:10   *those who are persecuted because of righteousness...*

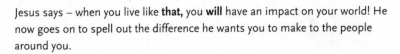

Jesus says – when you live like **that,** you **will** have an impact on your world! He now goes on to spell out the difference he wants you to make to the people around you.

3. SALT

Matthew 5:13

'You are the salt of the earth. But if the salt loses its saltiness, how can it be made salty again? It is no longer good for anything, except to be thrown out and trampled by men.'

If you think about it, it's probably no surprise that Jesus compares the impact he wants you to make with the impact that salt makes. Because whatever else you say about salt, **it always makes a difference to what you put it on!**

What sort of difference does salt make?

a)   It adds flavour

Whatever you put salt on – it makes a difference! Who would ever eat hot chips without salt? *(that's 'French Fries' for all our American friends!)* Or baked potatoes? Or peanuts? When you sprinkle salt on any food, you can instantly taste the difference. If you've ever had a mischievous friend sprinkle salt on your ice-cream, then you know it has an immediate impact!

b) It makes you thirsty

Have you ever been to your favourite hamburger restaurant, where the person who serves you puts **way too much** salt on your fries? Yuck! The only thing that you want to do after that is to drink stacks of water! Salt makes you thirsty! That's why bars always sell lots of salty snacks – peanuts, crisps, pretzels etc – because they know the salt will make you thirsty, and you'll end up buying more drinks!

c) It's a preservative

You might never have thought about this one. But food that has been salted lasts longer. Way back in the olden days – long before refrigeration – people would add salt to their meat to make it last longer. When the Europeans were off exploring the world in the 1700's – in those big tall sailing ships – they would keep meat, sprinkled heavily with salt, in barrels that could be kept for months. That's where we get meats like 'corned beef'. It simply means 'salted beef'.

d) Its power lies in its difference

No matter what reason you use salt, here is where its power lies. The basic power of salt to have an instant impact on anything it contacts is that it is **essentially different** from what you put it on. **If it wasn't different, it wouldn't make an impact!** If it wasn't different, it would be no use using it.

That's exactly what Jesus says.

Matthew 5:13
'You are the salt of the earth. But if the salt loses its saltiness, how can it be made salty again? It is no longer good for anything, except to be thrown out and trampled by men.'

'YOU ARE CALLED TO MAKE A DIFFERENCE BY BEING DIFFERENT'

What's the use of putting salt on your chips if the salt tastes exactly the same as the chips? And what's the use of salt that has lost its saltiness? What can you do with it? Add more salt? It's useless! May as well throw it out!

4. HOW TO MAKE A DIFFERENCE

In the same way, your life is meant to have an impact on those around you by being essentially **different** from everyone else. You have been called to live out the values of God's kingdom *(you know, 'blessed are the poor in spirit' – and all that)*. God wants to use you to **change** the lives of those around you. But to do that **you need to be different from them!**

There are two reasons why Christians can end up being very ineffective in this world.

> i. They stay together in their Christian huddle and never get out among the people who desperately need them *(more about that in the next chapter)*.

> ii. They get out among other people but are **essentially the same** as them – therefore they have no impact! *(this is the whole idea of 'salt')*.

Think about this: you are being called to **make** a difference by **being** different! You have a whole new set of values that reflects the very heart of Jesus. Is it possible that you're starting to lose your saltiness? Is it possible that in your attempt to be just the same as everyone else, you have lost your power to have a life-changing impact on those around you?

This world needs your 'salt'. You're meant to add flavour to what everyone else does. You have the ability to give purpose and depth to so many people around you who are purposeless and shallow.

This world needs your 'salt'. As you make your stand for Jesus, you can cause other people to be thirsty – thirsty for the lasting satisfaction that only Jesus can provide. In fact, the way you live your life can provoke other people to ask questions as they try to satisfy their deep inner thirst.

This world needs your 'salt'. You are a preservative that can stop people from crumbling away in a life without Jesus. You can offer the words of eternal life. You can direct them towards a saviour who can change their eternity. You can help them to believe in Jesus so that they *'will not perish but have everlasting life'* (John 3:16).

What an opportunity! You don't have to be a spiritual flight attendant or an ecclesiastical wrestlemania umpire who has zero impact on those around them! If you are a disciple, then Jesus calls you the *'salt of the earth'*. He wants you to go and make a difference. He has designed you to make a difference. He has filled you with his Spirit so that you have the **ability** to make a difference.

Do you know the most powerful weapon that you have? Do you know what will help your friends to see that Jesus can make a difference to their life? **It's when they see that Jesus has been powerful enough to change *your* life!**

So – today – whose life does he want you to go and make a difference in? Someone at home? Someone at school? Someone at work? One of your friends? Well – what are you waiting for? Off you go!

Are you still wondering whether you can really change them?

Check out the next chapter!

6 A DISCIPLE CHANGES LIVES

Matthew 5:14-16

1. LIVING IN A BLACKOUT

Have you ever been in a situation where there was **absolutely no light?**

It's a dark night – and all the electricity in your entire neighbourhood goes out. No TV – no computer – no lights – no nuffin! It's pitch black inside your house. Dad is stumbling around trying to find the torch in the garage. Mum is hunting around for those old candles which are stuck up the back of one of the kitchen cupboards. No one can find the matches and you keep tripping over the cat. No one can find

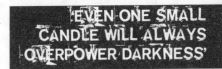

anything. Everyone's getting irritated with each other. No one knows how long it will last.

Has that ever happened to you? Absolutely no light? Irritating! Annoying! Maybe even a bit scary? No work gets done. No food gets cooked. No one knows what to do.

Imagine that the **whole world** went like that. For some reason, there was no more moon or stars at night. For some reason, the sun never rose each morning. There was no electricity. No battery power. No fire. The whole world was pitch black. No one could see.

That sounds like a description of the end of the world. Certainly, if that ever happened, the human race would not survive for very long!

Now, imagine that you have a match and a candle. Suddenly there is one light in this darkened world. Maybe not a very strong light, but at least it is a light.

Do you think anyone would notice? Do you think anyone would be paying attention to you? Do you think anyone would be helped by your light?

2. YOU ARE THE LIGHT OF THE WORLD

Darkness. That's a picture of what our world is like – **spiritually.** A world of blindness and darkness where people stumble about trying to make sense of the whole thing. And into this darkened world, Jesus has placed his disciples to be light to everyone around them. Imagine the difference that each disciple can make!

Listen to how Jesus describes **you!**

Matthew 5:14-16
'You are the light of the world. A city on a hill cannot be hidden. Neither do people light a lamp and put it under a bowl. Instead they put it on its stand, and it gives light to everyone in the house. In the same way, let your light shine before men, that they may see your good deeds and praise your Father in heaven.'

Disciples are described as being like *light*. Let's check out what light really does.

a) Helps you to see things clearly

Have you ever been on a *blind date*? You know – where you arrange to take someone out – and you don't know who they are – or what they look like – until you meet them?

I guess that's what being *blind* means. You can't see anyone. You don't know what's going on. Certainly – if someone is standing in the darkness – then you have no idea of what they are like. But as soon as they step into the light – well – that's what light does – it enables you to see things clearly. Try playing sport at night when there are no floodlights on the ground! You won't be able to see a thing!

b) Guides the way ahead

As well as helping you see things clearly, light also guides you on the way ahead.

Imagine your family is driving on a country road at night – and suddenly – your headlights go out! Aarrgghh!! You can't drive like this! All the lights might be on **in** the car – but if you can't see the way ahead, **you can't go ahead!**

c) Makes you feel safe

What's the difference between going for a walk in a lonely place during the day – and going to the same lonely place in the dark of night? I know there are parts of my city where I wouldn't be game to walk at night! I feel far safer when I'm walking in an area that has good streetlights. The explanation is very simple – light provides security.

d) Warns you of danger

You're walking along the road – and suddenly you see a whole string of vehicles passing you with bright flashing lights. Police cars, ambulances, fire-trucks. The flashing lights warn you that something is wrong.

e) The essential power of light

Let me show you why light is so powerful – **it always overcomes darkness!** Always, always, always! Darkness and light do not meet each other as equals. Light **always** wins.

Try an experiment. Have two rooms next to each other with a connecting door. Keep the door closed. Now make one room **completely dark** and then place a strong light in the other room. Got it? One completely dark room. One completely light room. With a closed door in between them.

Now open the door. What happens? Does the darkness come flooding into the lighted room and make it less light? **No way!** The lighted room does not lose any of its light by having the doorway to the darkened room opened.

But what happens in the darkened room? As soon as the door is opened, **light comes flooding in!** Even if the lighted room **only had a candle in it** – can you see that some of the light from that one little candle would penetrate the darkness and start to overcome it?

f) Overcoming darkness

Can you see that when Jesus describes you as *'the light of the world'*, he is saying something very powerful about you. Because, if you are *light* – then that means **you will always overcome darkness!**

'What – my little light?'

Yes! Your little light! Even one small candle will **always** overpower darkness. Light **always** overcomes darkness. That is the essential power of light. So no matter how dark things are around you – no matter what sort of 'deeds of darkness' everyone else is getting involved in – no matter how strong and powerful this world sometimes looks as it heads further and further away from Jesus – **God has placed you there to be his light in this darkened world!**

Maybe you're shining brilliantly – or maybe some of the stuff you're doing has clouded the light a little bit – but if you're a disciple – **Christ's light is shining through you!**

3. SO, WHERE ARE YOU SHINING YOUR LIGHT?

That's the key question: *'**Where** are you shining your light?* Look back at what Jesus says again:

> **Matthew 5:14-16**
> *'You are the light of the world. A city on a hill cannot be hidden. Neither do people light a lamp and put it under a bowl. Instead they put it on its stand, and it gives light to everyone in the house. In the same way, let your light shine before men, that they may see your good deeds and praise your Father in heaven.'*

THE KEY QUESTION: 'WHERE ARE YOU SHINING YOUR LIGHT?'

Jesus' words make sense. Imagine you have a super-powerful searchlight – able to illuminate the whole countryside. But instead of putting it up on a hill where it can help the whole town – instead of mounting it on a high stand to give it maximum penetration – you turn it on and hide it under a bucket!

That would be crazy! We have underground power lines – and underground phone cables – but imagine how stupid it would be if we had underground street lights! Or imagine we've had to install a new lighthouse to protect boats from being dashed to pieces on the rocks. How idiotic it would be to put the new lighthouse down a coal mine!

What's going to be the result if you turn on the brightest light and then hide it under a bucket? Two results come to mind:

a) There'll be lots of light **inside the bucket** (where it's not needed!)
b) There'll be no light at all getting **out where it is needed.**

Jesus is telling us something powerful here about how to be his disciple. He is not questioning how much light you have; he is not inquiring whether it's always as bright as it should be; he's certainly not questioning whether you have more or less light than the person next to you. But here's what he is definitely questioning: '**Where** are you shining it?'

This is always a danger for Christians. We get together with other Christians *(so far, so good!)*; we enjoy close community and awesome worship *(magnificent stuff!)*; we receive excellent Bible teaching and join fervent prayer times *(strongly recommended!)*.

Then we make the fatal mistake – **we stay there!** Rather than going out into the world that needs us – rather than getting alongside our non-christian friends who desperately need our light – rather than getting out as salt and light so that we make an impact on the world for Christ – we stay huddled together shining our lights brighter and brighter for each other.

We turn our churches into giant buckets to hide our lights under. We reduce our church youth groups and Christian schools into refuges where we shelter from the real world. We turn our Bible-study groups into holy huddles, and make sure we only have *good, safe Christian friends* at any social activity we join in.

The two results of all this ecclesiastical 'under-bucket' light-shining?

a) There's lots of light **inside the bucket** (where it's not needed!)
b) There's no light at all getting **out where it is needed.**

Of course you need to **start** by joining with your fellow Christians so you are consistently being fed and encouraged at church. And you need other Christians around you so that you don't end up compromising your stand by disobeying Jesus – and turning down the dimmer switch on your light.

But Jesus wants you to be a genuine disciple. He has designed you to make an impact on this world. He has designed you to be *'the salt of the earth'* so that by your very *difference* you can have a dramatic impact on anyone you meet. He has designed you to be *'the light of the world'* so that you can go out in a world of darkness and overcome it for eternity.

4. THE RESULTS OF SHINING OUR LIGHT 'OUT THERE'

Jesus spells out his action plan for you in the following verse:

Mathew 5:16
'In the same way, let your light shine before men, that they may see your good deeds and praise your Father in heaven.'

a)   Let your light shine before men ...

Christianity isn't meant to be a secret society. Christians aren't meant to be **so** mysterious that they hide everything they do as they sneak around like undercover cops. Look again at the words that Jesus uses to encourage us to shine our light where it is needed:

Matthew 5:14
'... A city on a hill cannot be hidden ...'

Matthew 5:15a
'Neither do people light a lamp and put it under a bowl ...'

Matthew 5:15b
'... Instead they put it on its stand, and it gives light to everyone in the house ...'

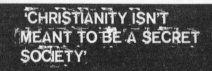
'CHRISTIANITY ISN'T MEANT TO BE A SECRET SOCIETY'

Mathew 5:16

'... let your light shine before men ...'

If Jesus has made a difference to you – **let the world know!** And the **reason** Jesus wants us to *'shine our light before others'*?

b) That they may see your good deeds ...

Jesus doesn't want us to hide the good we do – he wants it to be plain and obvious to everyone. He doesn't want us continually hiding back in the safety of church – he wants us out there making a difference.

c) And praise your father in heaven

And what's going to happen when we do that?

Matthew 5:16

'... that they may see your good deeds and praise your Father in heaven.'

We want to bring people to God. We don't want people to praise **us** – we want them to praise **God**. The way that people will know that Jesus has the power to change **their** life is when they see that his power is already changing **your** life.

And how do we live this radical obedience that has the power to change lives?

Next chapter!

45

'This book really helped me think about the commitment I made to God. Tim understands everything teenagers go through – all the things we struggle with. I can't wait to tell my friends what I learnt in this book'.

Rachel, Year 7

7 A WHOLE NEW WAY TO OBEY

Matthew 5:17-20

1. I WONDER WHAT I CAN GET AWAY WITH?

Have you ever asked that question? That is, you **sort of** want to obey someone, and you **more or less** want to do the right thing, but you don't **fully** want to comply – so you're wondering '*What can I get away with?*'

This often happens when you have a substitute teacher at school. Your regular teacher is away, and a brand new teacher appears in your classroom to look after you for that subject. C'mon – you **know** you are going to try and muck about and get away with anything you can! You're going to test this poor teacher to see what their breaking point is. I think that supply teachers must have a difficult life!

Many of the students at my church attend a nearby private school. Their winter school uniform includes the school blazer. There is also a school jumper they can wear if they want. But here's the deal – if they want to wear the school jumper (which is much more comfortable) – they have to wear the school blazer over the top! That's the school rule!

They **more or less** obey this uniform code, but you should see what happens once they get on the school bus! Once they get out of sight of their supervising teacher – and the bus pulls away – off come those blazers! In the safety of the school bus, they know they can get away with it!

'I wonder what I can get away with?'

You know that your dad and your mum will let you get away with different things. C'mon – you know their weak points and you relentlessly play them off against each other to get what you want.

Oh – don't look so innocent – I know you do it! If you want to stay out late, you know whether to ask your mum or your dad. If you want some extra money, you've worked out which one is the softer touch. If you're in trouble: you know the one you'd rather go to. You've worked out your parents – you know their strengths and their weaknesses – and you play them off against each other to see what you can get away with!

2. HOW FAR CAN I GO?

There is a different and more devious version of the 'What can I get away with' game. It's called 'How far can I go?'

That is – I'm not going to do the thing that is wrong, but how **close** can I get to doing the wrong thing without **actually** doing the wrong thing?

'How far can I go?'

This is the question that girls and guys so often ask when they're getting involved in a relationship.

'HOW FAR CAN I GO IN MY RELATIONSHIPS?'

I know what you mean when you ask that question. I think I asked the same question many years ago when I was first setting out on the glorious journey of discovering what a relationship with a girl could mean. Here's what I think you mean by that question:

'I know that there's some stuff that we could do together that would be completely wrong for two young people who are not married to each other. I know that God's word says that sexual intercourse is to be reserved for marriage, and that if we ever got involved like that it would be wrong. I understand that, and I'm never going to go that far in our relationship.

'But how far can I go?' We're not going to 'do it', but is it okay to get close? Is it okay to go further than kissing and cuddling? Is it okay to go groping and exploring? Is it okay to take some clothes off? Is it okay to go looking in places where we don't normally look? We're not going to have intercourse, but how far can we go?'

3. THE PROBLEM WITH THE QUESTION

I **understand** the question, but can you see there is something **basically wrong** with the question. *'How far can I go?'* means *'How close can I get to sinning?'* And whether you realise it or not, lying **behind** that question is this thought:

*'I want to enjoy the **fun** of sinning without **actually** sinning.'*

*'I want to sin just a **little** bit, but maybe not enough for it to count.'*

'I want to follow Jesus but I want to have a bit of fun on the side.'

Are you starting to see a problem with the question? Here's the difficulty:

Deep down you don't really want to obey what God has said – because you suspect it would be more fun to ignore him.

Ouch! That doesn't sound like *genuine obedience*. It's starting to sound a little more like *genuine disobedience*!

4. WHY DOES GOD HAVE ALL THOSE LAWS?

How do you feel when you look at all the laws and commands that God says we should obey? I'm sure there are times when you wish that he'd get rid of some of them!

*'Why do we have to have **ten** commandments? There's one or two that I'm not so keen on. Why can't we cut it back to seven? And what's the deal with calling them **commandments?** That's a bit old-fashioned, isn't it? Come on – this is the 21st century. Can't we modernise them and call them the ten **suggestions**?'*

There were certainly some people of Jesus' time that were hoping that he would get rid of all those old commands from God that they didn't like obeying. You can almost imagine their attitude. '*Now that Jesus is here – and wants to forgive people – do we even have to bother obeying God any more? C'mon, Jesus! You're going to get rid of all those commands and laws, aren't you?*'

5. WHAT JESUS SAYS ABOUT GOD'S LAW

Let's look at what Jesus says about God's law:

Matthew 5:17-18

'*Do not think that I have come to abolish the Law or the Prophets; I have not come to abolish them but to fulfil them. I tell you the truth, until heaven and earth disappear, not the smallest letter, not the least stroke of a pen, will by any means disappear from the Law until everything is accomplished.*'

Sounds like Jesus is taking God's law pretty seriously! He goes on:

Matthew 5:19-20

'*Anyone who breaks one of the least of these commandments and teaches others to do the same will be called least in the kingdom of heaven, but whoever practises and teaches these commands will be called great in the kingdom of heaven. For I tell you that unless your righteousness surpasses that of the Pharisees and the teachers of the law, you will certainly not enter the kingdom of heaven.*'

'JESUS WANTS TO TEACH YOU HOW TO HAVE GENUINE OBEDIENCE'

Can you see that Jesus is raising us to a very high standard. Jesus wants to get rid of the question '*What can I get away with?*'. He wants to get rid of the question '*How far can I go?*'

He wants to show you an entirely new way of obeying God's laws.

He wants to show you a way that will revolutionise everything about your Christian life. Jesus wants you to be a **genuine disciple**. Right now he wants to teach you how you can have **genuine obedience.**

8 TREATING PEOPLE RIGHT

Matthew 5:21-26

1. OUR WAY OF OBEYING RULES

Here's how obedience normally works. Someone in authority decides on a rule that we all have to stick to. It's like they put up a fence and say: *'Keep on this side of the fence. If you jump the fence, and cross over to the other side — you have broken the rule.'*

I think we all understand that. Anything that goes past the fence is wrong. Anything that leads up to the fence is okay.

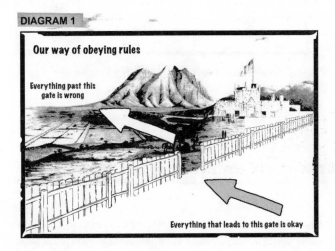

DIAGRAM 1

Our way of obeying rules

Everything past this gate is wrong

Everything that leads to this gate is okay

Every rule in the world is something like that. Whether it's a household rule that tells you what time you need to go to bed each night, or a sporting rule that tells you what's a fair way to tackle someone for the ball, or a school rule that tells you where out-of-bounds is, or a nation-wide rule that tells you how much tax you have to pay. They all work the same.

Let me show you with an easy example from our traffic rules. Lets say that the powers-that-be decide the speed limit is 60 mph. Here's how the rule works. Any speed that goes past the limit has broken the rule – any speed that stays this side of the limit is okay. So if I'm travelling at 80, or 70 or even 61, I have broken the rule. But if I'm travelling at 50, or 55 or even 60, I haven't broken the rule.

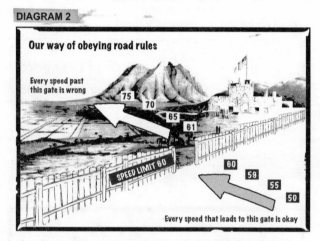

DIAGRAM 2

Our way of obeying road rules

Every speed past this gate is wrong
75 70 65 61
SPEED LIMIT 60
60 59 55 50
Every speed that leads to this gate is okay

That's the way every rule in the world works. No problems with that. But our problems start when we think that **God's rules** work the same way.

Listen in as Jesus describes a **whole new way** of obeying God!

2. THE COMMANDMENT ABOUT MURDER

a)   Our way of obeying

Matthew 5:21

'You have heard that it was said to the people long ago, 'Do not murder, and anyone who murders will be subject to judgment.''

So far so good. We know we're not allowed to murder anyone. We're all agreed on that. We know that anything that goes **'past the fence' of**

murder is wrong. But using our human logic, that means anything else that only leads up to it must be okay!

Is that right? You're not allowed to murder anyone, but as long as you don't actually end their life, it doesn't matter what you do to them? So it's okay to torture them, or hurt them, or abuse them, or humiliate them, or embarrass them, or yell at them...??

This is the way that the people of Jesus' time had interpreted God's law against murder.

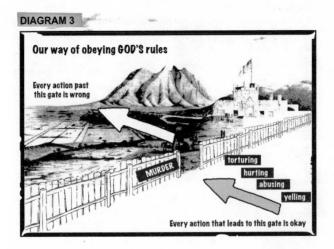

DIAGRAM 3

Our way of obeying GOD'S rules

Every action past this gate is wrong

MURDER

torturing
hurting
abusing
yelling

Every action that leads to this gate is okay

b)   God's way for us to obey

Matthew 5:21-22

'You have heard that it was said to the people long ago, `Do not murder, and anyone who murders will be subject to judgment.' But I tell you that anyone who is angry with his brother will be subject to judgment. Again, anyone who says to his brother, `Raca,' ['Worthless idiot!'] is answerable to the Sanhedrin. But anyone who says, `You fool!' will be in danger of the fire of hell.'

Jesus is showing us a **completely different** way of obeying God's rule. He is saying to us *'Because murder is wrong, you won't want to do **anything** that might lead to it. If the 'fence' of murder is wrong, then don't even get on the path that might lead to it!'*

'*Do not murder*' doesn't just mean '*Don't end someone else's life*'. The commandment against murder is meant to inspire us to see that because human life is so special, we wouldn't want to do **anything** that belittles or injures anyone else. If murdering someone is wrong, then it is also wrong to torture them, or hurt them, or abuse them, or humiliate them, or embarrass them, or yell at them...

In fact Jesus says: '*If you're angry with your brother, you will be subject to judgment*'. Why? Because anger is on the path that leads to murder. To make his point even more strongly, Jesus says that '*anyone who says, 'You fool!' will be in danger of the fire of hell.*' Why? Because treating someone as a fool –

'ANGER IS ON THE PATH THAT LEADS TO MURDER'

belittling them and humiliating them – is on the path that leads to murder. And if that path is only leading in one direction – **don't even get on it**!

c)   In fact – go even further

But Jesus has something more. He says: '*God's commandment against murder is not just meant to stop you doing negative things to other people – it's meant to inspire you to do positive things for them as well!*'

Matthew 5:23-24
'*Therefore, if you are offering your gift at the altar and there remember that your brother has something against you, leave your gift there in front of the altar. First go and be reconciled to your brother; then come and offer your gift.*'

The commandment against murder is meant to inspire you to go and fix up your relationships with other people! Right now, do you have a Christian brother or sister whom you've had a disagreement with? Are you in danger of starting down that dangerous path – to thinking of them as an 'idiot' and wounding them with hurtful words? God is saying there might be things you've got to fix up before you go any further.

Do you see how revolutionary God wants your obedience to be?

If you've got someone who's done the wrong thing by you – not only will you not murder them... not only will you not hurt them or abuse them or yell at them or blow them out... not only will you make sure you don't call them

DIAGRAM 4

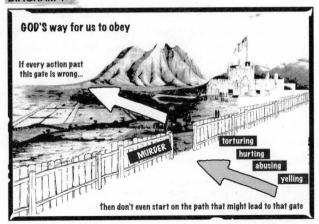

GOD'S way for us to obey

If every action past this gate is wrong...

MURDER

torturing
hurting
abusing
yelling

then don't even start on the path that might lead to that gate

names or treat them like an idiot... but you will go further than that! You will go and restore the relationship, and forgive them from your heart, and do whatever it takes so that the two of you can be brought back together again.

And the reason you will do that? Because that's the way that God treats you! He has sent his Son to die for you so that you can be brought back into an intimate relationship with him.

Do you see a whole new way of obeying God? Can you catch that there is a whole new level of obedience that he is raising you up to? If something is clearly sinful ... **you won't even get on the path that might lead you to it!**

9 TREATING SEX RIGHT

Matthew 5: 27-30

1. THE COMMANDMENT ABOUT ADULTERY

a) Our way of obeying

Okay – let's look at this next example.

Matthew 5:27

'You have heard that it was said, 'Do not commit adultery''.

Here's the way we **usually** interpret that commandment:

It's not hard to agree that *adultery* is a bad idea. That is, having sex with someone in a way that breaks a marriage bond – well, no one ever wins in that game. So far so good. We know we're not meant to have sex with someone we're not married to. We know that anything that goes 'past the fence' of adultery is wrong. But using our human logic, that means **anything else that only leads up to it must be okay!**

Is that right? You're not allowed to have sexual intercourse with someone you're not married to, but as long as you don't actually 'do it' , it doesn't matter what you do to them? So it's okay to be involved in petting, and fondling, and undressing, and groping, and looking... so long as you don't actually 'do it'?

This is the way that the people of Jesus' time had interpreted God's law against adultery. It's the same old question: *'How far can I go?'*

DIAGRAM 5

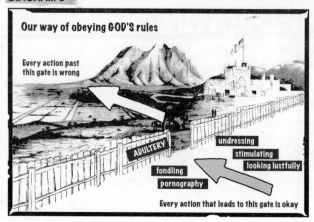

Our way of obeying GOD'S rules

Every action past this gate is wrong

ADULTERY

undressing
stimulating
looking lustfully
fondling
pornography

Every action that leads to this gate is okay

b) God's way for us to obey

Let's check out what Jesus does with that commandment. He is about to show us a whole new way to honour God with our obedience!

Matthew 5:27-28

'You have heard that it was said, `Do not commit adultery.' But I tell you that anyone who looks at a woman lustfully has already committed adultery with her in his heart.'

Jesus is showing us a **completely different way** of obeying God's rule. He is saying to us: *'Because adultery is wrong, you're not going to want to do **anything** that might lead to it. If the 'fence' of adultery is wrong, then don't even get on the path that might lead to it!'*

'Do not commit adultery' doesn't just mean *'Don't have sexual intercourse with someone you're not married to'*. The commandment against adultery is meant to inspire us to see that, because human sexuality is so special, we wouldn't want to do **anything** that cheapens it in any way. So if having sexual intercourse with someone you're not married to is wrong, then it is also wrong to fondle them, or grope them, or undress them, or look in places you're not meant to look...

In fact Jesus says *'whoever looks at a woman lustfully has already committed adultery with her in his heart.'* Why? Because looking lustfully (seeing someone – and wanting them in a wrong way – and even imagining in your mind how you'd do it) is on the path that leads to adultery. And if that path is only leading in one direction – **don't even get on it!**

DIAGRAM 6

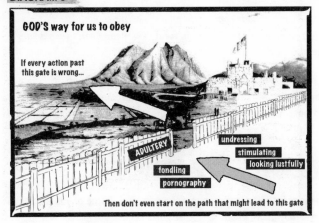

GOD'S way for us to obey

If every action past this gate is wrong...

ADULTERY

undressing
stimulating
looking lustfully
fondling
pornography

Then don't even start on the path that might lead to this gate

I remember some years ago I was reaching out to some students at the local high school. There were a number of boys in Year 10 who were interested in finding out about Jesus. We organised a 5-week *Discovering Jesus* course at lunchtime, and a number of students made the decision to follow Jesus.

I met up with the boys one week after they had made a commitment to Jesus. This was our first get-together now that they were Christians.

One of the boys, Brad, asked me an unusual question: *'Hey Tim, now that I'm a Christian, can I ask you something? One of my mates told me that now I'm a Christian, I'd have to stop sleeping with girls. Is that right?'*

'Oh!' I said. *'Yes – that's absolutely right! Did I forget to mention that last week?'* (loud groans from Brad!) *'So – now that you know that – do you still want to be a Christian?'*

Brad thought for a few minutes. *'Yep – I still want to be a Christian. And if I have to give up sleeping with girls until I'm married – I guess I can do it.'*

I thought to myself: *'Brad is making real progress'*. Then he floored me when he explained *'Well, I guess if I can't go out and 'do it' anymore, I'll have to content myself with just dreaming about it all day!'*

I took Brad to *Matthew 5: 27-28* (the verse that we've just looked at above) where he read the words ... *'anyone who looks at a woman lustfully has already committed adultery with her in his heart.'* An astonished look came over his face! *'You mean I can't even dream about it all day?'*

We laughed together. But Brad was learning something important about following Jesus. If having sexual intercourse with someone you're not married to is wrong, then it is also wrong to dream about it all day!

2. YOU'VE GOT TO BE JOKING!

Let's just press the pause button for a moment. Some of you are thinking: *'I can't even daydream about it? You've gotta be joking! How can I help but think about it? Tim – you're just an old geezer. You're over 50 now. What would you understand about teenage sexuality?'*

I understand what you are going through with sexual temptation. I know what it's like to feel trapped inside an almost adult body, where you feel absolutely controlled by an extremist army of feral hormones which have gone ballistic as they race and throb throughout every extremity of your body, and try and convince you that you are a helpless prisoner-of-war in a battle where sexuality has conquered you and you must give in to its every demand!

Sometimes you feel like you will **explode** if you don't do something about this sexual tension which is rising up and pulsating within you.

> **'NO ONE HAS EVER DIED BECAUSE THEY EXPLODED THROUGH NOT RELEASING THEIR SEXUAL URGES'**

I have some good news for you. *No one has ever died because they exploded through not releasing their sexual urges*!

But your body might fool you into thinking that it will!

The police have never been called to investigate such a death or written in their report: *'The death was caused by an explosion resulting from the fact that they didn't release their sexual tension!'*.

Your body might scream at you to say *'I've got to give in to those sexual urges!'* Do you know what Jesus says?

1 John 4:4
' The spirit who is in you is greater than the spirit who is in the world.'
[see footnote]

James 4:7
'Resist the devil, and he will flee from you.'

I know how you feel, **but who are you going to believe?** Your body says to you: 'You've got to get involved sexually', but Jesus says to you: 'I've got something *far better* in mind for your sexuality. And I have given you my Spirit that you might have the strength to obey me!' There's a whole new level of joyful obedience that he wants to lift you up to.

3. GO EVEN FURTHER

Jesus cares so much that you don't get on that path that takes you closer to sin – that he says: '*Do **anything** it takes so that you don't head down that path!*'

Matthew 5:29-30
'If your right eye causes you to sin, gouge it out and throw it away. It is better for you to lose one part of your body than for your whole body to be thrown into hell. And if your right hand causes you to sin, cut it off and throw it away. It is better for you to lose one part of your body than for your whole body to go into hell.'

Now just before you rush off to the kitchen drawer to find a sharp knife – take a moment to understand what Jesus is saying. **Jesus does not mean that you should take him absolutely physically, literally at this point!** He is using a **vivid story** – an extreme story – to make an **important point.**

Jesus doesn't want you to cut off any part of your body just because it causes you to sin. If we all did that, we wouldn't have very many appendages left on our body!

What he is saying is this: '*Do anything it takes to deal with the temptation that is dragging you down now*'.

If you're looking at something or someone and that's causing temptation for you – then **stop looking**. If there's a web-site that causes you to start down that path – **don't go there**. If there are magazines or DVDs that start you in that direction – **burn them**. If there's something wrong happening with your boyfriend or girlfriend right now – then **stop seeing them** until you can clear it up.

Jesus is calling you to a new level of obedience. Jesus is calling you to have a genuine obedience. He has given you his Spirit to live in you so that you might be able to enjoy living your life the way that God says.

Here's the choice: You can either obey God reluctantly ... and try to get away with everything you can... and try and get as close to sinning as you possibly can...

That is not genuine obedience!

Or you can obey God joyfully... knowing that if he's said something is wrong – then you don't even want to get on the path that might lead you towards that sin.

That is genuine obedience! That is the standard that Jesus is calling you to.

Jesus gives stacks of other examples of the two different ways of obeying God.

1. DIVORCE

Matthew 5:31-32
'It has been said, 'Anyone who divorces his wife must give her a certificate of divorce.' But I tell you that anyone who divorces his wife, except for marital unfaithfulness, causes her to become an adulteress, and anyone who marries the divorced woman commits adultery.'

Jesus is not having a shot at someone just because they're divorced. The Bible acknowledges that marriage sometimes breaks down, and then we reluctantly recognise this with divorce.

But here's what he is saying. The allowance of divorce in the Bible is a **reluctant concession**. It's something that unfortunately happens **when everything else has been tried.**

This is what some people in Jesus' day were doing – they were looking for an easy option. Rather than working through the hard slog of trying to restore a relationship, some people were just racing out and getting divorced the first time something went wrong with their marriage.

Divorce is only there as the last resort – and it is never what God has in mind when two people marry. This is a whole new way to obey God!

2. MEANING WHAT YOU SAY

Matthew 5:33
'Again, you have heard that it was said to the people long ago, 'Do not break your oath, but keep the oaths you have made to the Lord.''

You know what people were doing? They would say: '*I swear to God that this is true!*' And they thought: '*If I swear an oath to God, then I have to tell the truth.*' But they **then** said: '*If I **don't** swear an oath to God – then I can tell as many lies as I like!*'

Jesus says '*No!*' That's just trying to see what you can get away with! The command about oaths was meant to inspire you to even greater levels of truthfulness!

Jesus clarifies it with this statement:

Matthew 5:37
'*Simply let your 'Yes' be 'Yes,' and your 'No,' 'No'; anything beyond this comes from the evil one.*'

Jesus' message? Tell the truth. Mean what you say. Don't try and get out of it!

3. GETTING EVEN

Matthew 5:38
'*You have heard that it was said, 'Eye for eye, and tooth for tooth.''*

This was indeed one of God's commands from way back in the Old Testament. And the people of Jesus' day were taking it absolutely literally! So if your neighbour came over and punched out one of your teeth, you made sure you went over and knocked one of his teeth out as well!

Jesus says: '*You don't understand! That's not the way I want you to obey! That's not the way I want you to treat people!*'.

God originally gave that law to **limit** people paying each other back. What used to happen was this: one of your neighbours might come over and steal one of your cows. So you would go over and steal **ten** of his cows. Then he would get all his brothers together and come over and burn all your fields. So you'd go over and flatten his house. Then he'd come over and kill all your family! So God said: *'Stop! Keep it fair. Limit your revenge. Simply make it 'an eye for an eye and a tooth for a tooth!'*

Jesus now says: *'You can go further than that! You don't **have** to pay back. You don't have to extract revenge at all! In fact – this whole command was meant to inspire you to even higher levels of obedience!'*

Matthew 5:39-41
'If someone strikes you on the right cheek, turn to him the other also. And if someone wants to sue you and take your tunic, let him have your cloak as well. If someone forces you to go one mile, go with him two miles'

Jesus gives us a whole new way of obeying! If you've got an enemy – don't plot how

'OVERWHELM EVIL WITH GOOD'

to get them back. Outrageously give to them – and bless them beyond belief. Give them far more than they deserve! Overwhelm evil with good!

4. DEALING WITH YOUR ENEMIES

Matthew 5:43-44
'You have heard that it was said, 'Love your neighbour and hate your enemy.' But I tell you: Love your enemies and pray for those who persecute you.'

God had often said *'Love your neighbour'* but he had **never** said: *'Hate your enemies'*! People had just added this in over the years. *'Well, I guess I have to love people who are my friends. But there's no way I'm going to love anyone who's my enemy!'*

Jesus gives us a whole new way of obeying him. Don't hate your enemies – **love your enemies!**

And look at how radical his call to obedience is!

Matthew 5:46-47
'If you love those who love you, what reward will you get? Are not even the tax collectors doing that? And if you greet only your brothers, what

I know it's easy just to hang out with your friends. To only love those who love you. To only love those who are easy to love. But here, Jesus is saying: *'If you only hang out with the kids who hang out with you – if you only care about the kids who care about you... what's so special about that? Even non-Christians do that!'*

That's not the love that Jesus says will change the world. That's not the obedience that Jesus says will change the world. What would happen if you hung out with the kids that no one wants to hang out with? What would happen if you showed some loving care to someone who was giving you a hard time?

Jesus says: *'I have something much bigger in mind for you'*. He is calling you to genuine obedience.

5. TWO WAYS OF OBEYING

There are two ways to try to obey God. Only one of them is what Jesus is really after.

1. You can obey God **reluctantly**.

2. Or you can obey him **joyfully**.

Lets look at that another way:

1. You can obey him cos you **have to**.

2. Or you can obey him cos you **want to**.

You can try and see how close you can go to sinning – and see how much you can get away with. Or you can determine that if God has clearly set out a sin – you're not even going to start on the path that might take you there.

You can say to God *'I guess I'll obey you, but I wish I didn't have to keep your stupid rules'*. Or you can say to God *'What do you want me to do today? I want to go wherever you take me!'*

Only one of these is genuine obedience.

The other is counterfeit obedience.

Think about your life. Where are you trying to get around what God has commanded? Where are you seeing what you can get away with? Where are you in danger of defying God right now?

That area where you're trying to get away with stuff ... that area where you're going right to the very edge – you know it's dangerous to hang around the edge of a cliff. One puff of wind – and over you go. Maybe even right now you know you're on the edge, and you feel you're about to fall.

Jesus wants you back! Sure – obeying God can be hard. **But it's good!**

Imagine your sports team has played hard all year. You've made it to the final and you're up against a tough opposition. You've played a gruelling match and it's gone all the way to the end and you've finished up dead even. The game has been forced into extra time, and with all this additional effort, you're feeling absolutely exhausted. In the dying seconds of the game, your team finally scores the decider, and you finish the match as the victorious premiers.

Every ounce of energy has been drained from your body. All you want to do is collapse into a hot bath and never run again! Your team is presented with a giant shield – it takes your whole team to lift it – and despite your exhaustion, you hold it high and celebrate your moment of triumph.

But all around the stadium, the crowd is cheering for you. So holding your Championship Shield high, you start off on your victory lap. Exhausted? Absolutely! Is that shield heavy? You bet ya! **But there's no way you're going to miss out on your victory lap**. You might feel worn out, but this is your moment of triumph!

As a Christian, you are on your victory lap. Jesus has won the battle, and you're a player on his side. He has defeated the devil and the devil's entire team. He gives you this victory for you to enjoy. You may be exhausted, but you're proudly running around the stadium with the shield of obedience held high.

Imagine you've won that Grand Final. And it's now time for the victory celebrations. But rather than joining in with your mates, you go off with the opposition. You join in **their** party. And you blow out **your own team!**

That's crazy! But sometimes as Christians we do just that. Jesus has won the victory – and you're on his winning team. But maybe right now you're off with the opposition, doing it their way.

JESUS HAS WON THE BATTLE, AND YOU ARE ON THE VICTORY LAP

Jesus is calling you to a new, genuine obedience. He's got a whole new way for you to obey and serve God. He's on his victory lap – and he wants you to run with him.

Right now, Jesus is calling you to genuine obedience. When he calls, will you come?

11 'ME' WORSHIP

1. 'ME' SPORT

Have you ever played sport alongside someone who was just out there for themselves? It's horrible. They hog the ball. They never pass. They show off to the spectators. They never back you up. They never do any of the hard slog.

If you've got a sporting team that's full of players who are mainly there just for themselves – it'll never work. The team will end up being destroyed.

Cos you're either mainly in it for the team – or you're mainly in it for yourself.

2. 'ME' RELATIONSHIPS

Have you ever been in a relationship where you eventually worked out that the other person was in it mainly for their own benefit, and not for you? That can be pretty devastating. Maybe it's really happened to you. You were in a committed relationship with someone – and you really cared about them, and you thought they cared about you, but after a while you worked out that they were only interested in what they could get out of you.

You didn't matter in the end. They got what they wanted – and they didn't really care about you.

And maybe you were hurt. Maybe you were used. Maybe you were abused.

Eventually you can always spot it. If the relationship goes for long enough, you can usually work out whether someone's in the relationship for you, or for themselves. And if people are only in it for themselves, then it's never going to work.

3. 'ME' CHRISTIANITY

Are you involved in Christian activities? Do you go to a church youth group with lots of your friends? Perhaps you're in a small Bible-study group with some other people about your age. Or perhaps you love joining in with the whole congregation at church on Sunday.

Do you get to go away on Christian camps? Does your youth group have outings and activities? Have you ever got involved in a work project – where you went out and helped someone less fortunate than yourself? Perhaps you've even gone away on a mission trip?

Do you do some of these things? They all sound like great things! But if you're involved in any Christian activities, I have a question I'd like to ask you.

Why?

Now I know, there is always a mixture of reasons as to why you would get involved in a Christian activity. Probably stacks of good explanations as to why you would go to your church youth group. A variety of motives why you would go away on a camp.

Or join a Bible-study group. Or go to church.

But what's the **main** reason? When it all boils down, what's your main motivation? Can I suggest that your main reason for doing any Christian activity will probably fall into one of two categories:

- You'll either mainly do it for Jesus and his team.
- Or you'll mainly do it for yourself.

There is a huge difference between the two!

4. DOING THE RIGHT THINGS FOR THE WRONG REASONS

You can actually end up doing the right thing – for the **wrong** reason. You can end up doing Christian things – **but mainly doing it just for yourself.**

What do you mean?

Your favourite band is leading worship at church. So you go down the front and join in 'the pit' with everyone else – jumping and dancing and yelling out the words of the song.

Maybe it's your favourite song. **But what happens when it's not one of your favourites?** You know – a song that other people might like, but it just doesn't do that much for you. Do you still join in? Do you still praise God just as enthusiastically?

Or is it possible that as you stop moshing around,

'YOU CAN END UP DOING THE RIGHT THING – FOR THE WRONG REASON'

and slink back into the 'uninvolved' section of the crowd, that you might just grumble to the person next to you in despair and complain: *'I don't know how anyone could like this stupid song!'*

You can end up doing Christian things – but doing it just for yourself.

You're there at your Bible study every week. You hardly ever miss a week. But deep down you're there because they're a good bunch of friends. And while you're with all your friends – that's cool. And while you're with your favourite leader – that's cool.

But if your favourite leader changes and can no longer continue... or you're not put with **all** your best friends – do you stay involved? Or do you sink back to a position where you can't be bothered going?

You can end up doing Christian things – but doing it just for yourself.

'How was church last night?'

'Well, I didn't get much out of it!'

I understand that. Sometimes **I** don't get a whole lot out of a particular church service, or a particular sermon!

But is that why you are there? So that you could get something out of it? Are you there mainly for yourself, or are you there mainly for Jesus and his team?

You can end up doing Christian things – but doing it just for yourself.

So far, we're learning some awesome things about being genuine disciples. We've already looked at how to have genuine success. We've just discovered how to have genuine obedience. Right now, Jesus wants to teach us about genuine worship.

'JESUS WANTS TO TEACH US ABOUT GENUINE WORSHIP'

Because in Jesus' day, there were plenty of people who were really getting into this 'discipleship' thing. They were there at church, they'd be singing and dancing, getting into their bibles, praying great prayers, being generous in their giving, lots of money in the offering – and man! – everyone else just looked up to them and admired them.

They were the super-Christians!

But Jesus turns the blowtorch of his word on them and says :*'Some of you are doing lots of spiritual things – but deep down- you're just doing it for yourselves.'*

Get ready to have your life of worship turned upside down!

12 DANGEROUS WORSHIP   Matthew 6:1

1. YOU GET THE REWARD YOU'RE AFTER

Jesus starts Matthew chapter 6 with a warning:

> **Matthew 6:1**
> *'Be careful not to do your 'acts of righteousness' before men,
> to be seen by them. If you do, you will have no reward
> from your Father in heaven'*

There is a huge warning from Jesus. You can do lots
of things which look really Christian, and look like
you're pumping away at your worship of God. You can be a champion prayer – a great speaker – a hot musician – an understanding counsellor – an
enthusiastic worshipper – a generous giver – a daily Bible reader...

You can do all that – but you can do it **just for yourself** – to make yourself feel
good.

Just to make everyone else sit up and notice and say *'Boy – he's doing well at
being a Christian'.*

> One of our teenagers at our church came up to me one Sunday night,
> and as I was chatting with him, he said to me: *'I've been working hard
> at spending time with God – reading my Bible and praying. I've spent the
> last 150 days having a 'quiet time' **without missing a day!'***
>
> I was proud of him! This sounded like a magnificent effort. It was
> certainly better than what I had been doing! But I had one small worry
> (which I kept to myself): *'I wonder why he told me?'*

> **Matthew 6:1 again**
> *'Be careful not to do your 'acts of righteousness' before men to be seen by*

them. If you do, you will have no reward from your Father in heaven'

Jesus is showing us an important principle: **'You get the reward you're after'**.

That is, you might be a faithful Christian, humbly serving Jesus, reaching out to others, genuinely seeking to please God, and whether anyone around you ever notices you or not – you simply want to be the person that God has designed you to be.

Is that the reward you're after? That quietly you will show that you really belong to God? Jesus says: *'If that's what you're after – that's what you'll get.'*

'YOU GET THE REWARD YOU'RE AFTER'   But Jesus also says: *'If you're doing lots of Christian things – and the main reason you're doing it is so other people will notice you – and be impressed by you – and say 'My goodness he's doing well as a Christian'* ...

If that's what you're after – that's what you get **and nothing else.** There is no need for God to reward you.

Does this make sense? **You get the reward you're after**. If you truly want to please God – then that's what will happen. But if you mainly want to impress other people – if that's your **real** motivation – then that's all that's going to happen.

2. SO, WHOSE APPROVAL DO YOU WANT?

When I was a young Christian – around 20 years old – late one night as I was driving home from our church youth group, on the edge of the darkened street I noticed a young man who was lying in the gutter. I pulled over to see what the problem was, and it didn't take long to work out – he was drunk! Very drunk!

He wasn't able to say anything coherent, so I reached into his pocket, and in his wallet I found his I.D. He lived locally, so I decided I would drive him home.

I lifted him into my van – put a seat belt on him – and then walked around to my driver's door. By the time I got in, his excess of alcohol had played violent tricks with his digestive system, and he had emptied the entire contents of his stomach all over the front seat of my car! Yuck!

Anyway – I got him out – I cleaned him up – I cleaned my car up – and gave the whole thing a second shot. I drove him to his house – there was someone home – and I delivered him safely to his front door. I then drove off on my merry way.

As I drove home, a strange sequence of thoughts entered my head. *'What I did tonight was really good. Picking up that drunk was the Christlike thing to do.'*

Now it was the **next thought** that had me worried. I said to myself: *'I can't wait to get to church on Sunday so I can tell everyone what I did!'*

Then I thought about it for a while. *'Why was I so keen to tell everyone else?'* **Because I wanted them to know how good I was!**

Hmmm. I was being challenged in my motivation. Was I happy to do what was Christlike – **because** it was Christlike – **or did I really just want everyone else to praise me?**

I worked out that I simply wanted to do what was right. It would be unhelpful in the extreme to try and get everyone else to think how good I was. So I decided I wouldn't tell anyone. Not a word. *(Yeah, yeah, I know I've just told **you** – but it happened over 30 years ago – and you probably don't know me anyway – so I think it'll be okay!)*

Anyway, **then** I started to think: *'Gee, I'm good for not telling anyone!'*

3. THE CRY OF YOUR HEART

Do you see the problem? Anytime you do something good – anytime you do something Christlike – anytime you're involved in any act of Christian worship or charity – there's always the danger that you could end up doing the **right** thing for the **wrong** reason.

This is dangerous worship!

"ME' WORSHIP IS DANGEROUS WORSHIP!

Here's why – because God knows the real cry of your heart. Your **words** might be saying: '*O Jesus, I love you*' ... But if deep down you're secretly thinking: '*I hope everyone else notices how well I'm doing at this Jesus thing*'... then that's the real cry of your heart. And that's all you're going to get. Everyone will notice you. And God won't notice you at all.

Let's look at three ways to avoid this 'dangerous worship'. Yep – they're in the next chapter!

13 A WHOLE NEW WAY TO WORSHIP

Matthew 6:9-13

1. BEING GENEROUS

Jesus' first example of 'a new way to worship' has to do with **being generous.**

Matthew 6:2-4

'So when you give to the needy, do not announce it with trumpets, as the hypocrites do in the synagogues and on the streets, to be honoured by men. I tell you the truth, they have received their reward in full. But when you give to the needy, do not let your left hand know what your right hand is doing, so that your giving may be in secret. Then your Father, who sees what is done in secret, will reward you.'

You know how it works. Someone comes up to you in the street, and they're collecting for a worthy cause. Or you see an ad on TV asking you to support a welfare organisation. Or someone calls to your door – they're collecting for a great charity that helps thousands of people.

What are you going to do? How much are you going to give? **And who's going to see you?**

You need to understand what was happening in Jesus' day. Some of the very religious people used to walk the streets looking for someone to help. Someone who needed a handout. Someone who needed a cash donation.

And as they walked around – being very important people – they used to have a 'group' that paraded with them – their servants – their underlings – their professional groupies. And whenever one of these religious people would stop to help a beggar, it almost turned into a circus. Their professional groupies would stop – gather a crowd around – announce the whole thing with a few blasts on the trumpet – and when everyone was watching, they would make a loud announcement:

'Ladies and gentlemen, your favourite rabbi – Rabbi Benjamin – will now show why he is one of Israel's most generous people! Watch carefully as he places a golden coin in this poor beggar's plate! O, ladies and gentlemen – what a generous act! How about a round of applause for the godly, the generous, the one and only – Rabbi Benjamin!'

(Well, maybe it didn't happen **exactly** like that, but do you get the point?)

'DON'T DO IT FOR YOURSELF – DO IT FOR GOD'

Jesus is saying – being generous is good, but if you're going to do it – **don't make a song and dance about it!** Don't draw people's attention to it! Don't hog the limelight!

Don't do it for yourself – cos that's the only reward you'll get! Do it for God – and then your heavenly Father will reward you.

It's all a matter of which reward you really want.

2. DENYING YOURSELF

One of the common practices of God's people throughout the ages has been **fasting**. Going without food for a time. Not to lose weight on a diet. Not to raise money for a charity. But simply to deny yourself some pleasure – and to help you focus on God. When fasting is mentioned in the Bible, it is usually associated with praying. God's people sometimes fast to help them with their prayer. It's a great way to worship God!

This next example of 'a new way to worship' has to do with **fasting.**

Matthew 6:16-18
'When you fast, do not look sombre as the hypocrites do, for they disfigure their faces to show men they are fasting. I tell you the truth, they have received their reward in full. But when you fast, put oil on your head and wash your face, so that it will not be obvious to men that you are fasting, but only to your Father, who is unseen; and your Father, who sees what is done in secret, will reward you.'

Once again, some of the religious heavyweights wanted people to know how godly they were at denying themselves pleasure. When they were fasting

– they longed for the whole world to know! So what they would do is get cosmetics, and charcoal and other things they could smear on their face, and they would disfigure themselves. Make themselves look haggard and ugly. Make themselves look thin and gaunt. Make themselves look sickly. Make themselves look humble and lowly.

Then everyone could gasp in admiration and exclaim: *'Look at how haggard Rabbi Benjamin looks! Check out his face! He is fasting so much that he is looking sick! O – poor man ! Can we help him? If only we could be as godly as he is!'*

'YOUR FATHER, WHO SEES WHAT IS DONE IN SECRET, WILL REWARD YOU'

Jesus says: *'That's not genuine worship. When you fast – look your best! Make sure no one knows that you're doing it! Don't do it for yourself – cos that's the only reward you'll get! Do it for God – and then your heavenly father will reward you.*

It's all a matter of which reward you really want.

3. PRAYING

Jesus gives one more example of 'a new way to worship'. *(I have kept it till last cos it's so important!)* Jesus goes to the very core of Christian worship – **praying**. And yes – once again – the religious hotshots of his day had managed to turn this very godly exercise into a publicity stunt for themselves.

a) Don't be like the hypocrites
Matthew 6:5-6
> *'And when you pray, do not be like the hypocrites, for they love to pray standing in the synagogues and on the street corners to be seen by men. I tell you the truth, they have received their reward in full. But when you pray, go into your room, close the door and pray to your Father, who is unseen. Then your Father, who sees what is done in secret, will reward you.'*

Same deal. Religious people would go around with their groupies – pick a popular street corner, make an announcement, gather a crowd – and then when all their admiring onlookers had assembled, they would spout forth an eloquent prayer that everyone could admire and wonder at how holy they must really be.

Jesus says: *'That's not genuine worship. When you pray – don't make a song and dance about it! If you need to – do it in secret so that only your heavenly father knows.'*

Don't do it for yourself – because that's the only reward you'll get! Do it for God – and then your heavenly father will reward you.

It's all a matter of which reward you really want.

And because prayer is so important, Jesus now has some extra instructions to help us to be genuine.

b)   Don't be like the pagans
Matthew 6: 7-8
'And when you pray, do not keep on babbling like pagans, for they think they will be heard because of their many words. Do not be like them, for your Father knows what you need before you ask him.'

It's not just Christians who pray. All sorts of people in all sorts of religions pray. In fact, some people just babble on meaninglessly – thinking that the more words they pray –the more their 'god' will listen.

Jesus says *'That's not genuine worship. You don't have to pray thousands of meaningless words. You don't have to convince God by going on and on and on and on and on and on and on! Your father in heaven already knows what you need!'*

Do you sometimes think your prayers might have become *meaningless words*?

Think back to when you were younger. You know, a little kid. You're playing at home on a hot summer day when the ice cream van pulls up outside your house. You hear the bell ringing, and neighbourhood kids are coming out to buy their ice creams.

You'd like to eat an ice cream too – so you go to your dad to ask if he can give you the money to buy one. Can you imagine asking like this?

'O father – you who are the ruler of this household – you who are my master and commander – I beg that you would look upon my distress in the heat of this day. O father – I do not deserve anything from you – and I know I don't even deserve to talk with you. But I pray from the bottom of my heart that you would extend your favour to me and grant me this simple request.

O father – I humbly ask that from your bounty and from your generosity, that you would provide that golden coin that is required for my needs to be satisfied. I do not deserve to be your child – I know I have no foundation for asking for such a blessing, but I beg, I implore, I beseech you that you would extend this favour to me by granting this humble request from your lowly servant for one lick of an ice confection.'

That's not the way kids talk to their dads! You don't need to use meaningless words. Especially when your dad probably already knows that you'd like an ice cream!

Jesus says: 'You don't have to pray thousands of meaningless words. Your father in heaven already knows what you need!'

You mean that right now, God already knows what I need? He sure does! Right now, if you need to be comforted, then God already knows that. Right now, if you need guidance for the future, God already knows that. Right now, if you genuinely need money for something worthwhile, God already knows that. All you have to do is ask! Don't babble on like the pagans! Pray to your Father in heaven!

But **how** do I pray to my Father in heaven? How do I declare to him 'the cry of my heart'? Next chapter!

14 THE CHALLENGE TO BE DIFFERENT

Matthew 6: 9-13

1. DIFFERENT FROM THE WORLD

If you're looking carefully at Matthew Chapter 6, you're probably noticing a recurring theme in everything Jesus is saying. See if you can spot it:

6:2 *'So when you give to the needy, do not announce it with trumpets, as the hypocrites do...'*

6:5 *'And when you pray, do not be like the hypocrites...'*

6:7 *'And when you pray, do not keep on babbling like pagans...'*

6:8 *'Do not be like them...'*

6:16 *'When you fast, do not look sombre as the hypocrites do...'*

It's all summarised in **verse 8:** '*Do not be like them*'. It is almost a theme verse for this whole book. It is the cry of **Jesus'** heart – a call for genuine disciples to be **different** from everyone else in the world.

Do you want to know how to be a genuine disciple for Jesus on this planet? Do you want to know how to accomplish the mission that he has set out for you? Do you want to know how to be a positive influence on your friends so that they might be changed to follow Jesus?

Jesus is calling you to be radically different from those around you who don't honour him. You are not to have the same values as your friends at school. You are not to have the same cheap relationships as your mates do. You are not to disrespect your parents the way everyone else does. You are not to trash your sexuality the way the cool crowd does.

You are being called to have an integrity which is radically different. You are being called to have a lifestyle that is radically different. You are being called to have a radically different obedience; a different worship; a different prayer life;

a radically different everything!

Oh – you're meant to be out there in the world to make a change for Jesus! You're meant to be out there in your school so that other students will discover the difference that Jesus makes. You're not meant to withdraw and hide out in your own little Christian club. Jesus wants you out there cos there's a world that needs to be changed.

But the way you're gonna change it is by being essentially different from the values of those who are around you!

'JESUS IS CALLING YOU TO BE RADICALLY DIFFERENT FROM THOSE AROUND YOU'

There it is in verse 8: *'Do not be like them'*.

The Christian church is strong and it is powerful when it is full of disciples who are radical in being **different** from the sinful world around them. And the Christian church is weak and ineffective when it is essentially the **same** as the sinful world around them.

The same is true for your church youth group. Or the Christians at your school. Or your small Bible-study group. Or your church sporting team.

You will be strong and powerful when you are **different** from the sinful world around you. You will be weak and ineffective when you are essentially the **same** as the sinful world around you.

2. DIFFERENT IN OUR PRAYER

Jesus is saying: *'Don't be like the rest of the world in any way! But particularly, do not be like them in their prayers'*. This matters so much to Jesus, that he now goes on to show us the **right** way to pray. The **genuine** way to pray.

Here's how to have an awesome prayer life. If you look at **Matthew 6:9**, you might even recognise the prayer that Jesus is about to teach us:

> **Matthew 6:9**
> *'Our Father in heaven, hallowed be your name... '*

Sound familiar? Learn that somewhere? It's the most well-known prayer in the bible. It's called **'The Lord's Prayer'**.

Now I want you to notice something crazy here. Jesus has just instructed us not to be like the pagans, who pray meaningless words to God without thinking. Okay – got it? No more meaningless words! He then shows us an alternative – 'The Lord's Prayer'.

Now here's the crazy bit. **If there's one prayer that is mumbled meaninglessly around the world – this is it!**

Have you ever been in church when the whole congregation prays the Lord's Prayer? Talk about meaningless mumbling! When my kids went to primary school, on official occasions, they always sang 'The School Song' and mumbled 'The School Prayer'. What was the School Prayer? **The Lord's Prayer!**

The Lord's Prayer is mumbled meaninglessly thousands of times around the world every day! Jesus didn't give us this prayer so we would have a new way of mumbling! He gave it to us **so that our prayers would be genuine!** It's a way of checking what it is that we actually pray about!

If you want to check whether you're into this Jesus thing for yourself – or for the honour of Jesus – check what you pray about. Because often our prayers are just like a shopping list of demands that we want for ourselves!

'Dear Lord.
Please get me a boyfriend (or a girlfriend, as the case my be!).
Please get me a good exam result.
Please get me a good job.
Please give me lots of money.'
 'C'mon Jesus!
Go fetch!
Roll over!
Play dead!
Good Jesus!'

Jesus didn't give us the Lord's Prayer to give us something to mumble about. He gave it to us **to radically change what we pray about.** Notice, he never said: *'Pray this prayer'* (that is, repeat these exact words). He said in **verse 9:** *'This, then, is **how** you should pray'*. Or in other words – *'These are the sorts of things you should pray about'*.

So – do you want to know what to pray about? Here's the guide from the master himself.

3. A WHOLE NEW APPROACH

a) Pray for God's honour

Matthew 6:9
'Our Father in heaven, hallowed be your name'

A great way to start your prayers is to pray for God's honour. Praise him for who he is! Honour him as your great King!

Is this the way you usually start your prayers?

b) Pray for God's kingdom

Matthew 6:10
'your kingdom come, your will be done on earth as it is in heaven.'

Jesus wants us to centre our prayers on God's kingdom. To pray that God's kingdom will be present here on earth. To pray that we will run things here in a way that reflects God's kingdom.

c) Pray for God's provision

Matthew 6:11
'Give us today our daily bread.'

I must confess, I tend to **start** my prayers by just asking God for things – rather than praying to honour him, or praying for his kingdom! But there is certainly a time to place your requests before God. He loves to hear us ask – and he loves to answer. We need to live our whole lives acknowledging that God is the one who provides everything.

d) Pray for God's forgiveness

Matthew 6:12
'Forgive us our debts, as we also have forgiven our debtors.'

When we come before God, we come as people who

need his forgiveness. We need to confess our sins and ask for his cleansing. This is a very humbling way to pray!

e) Pray for God's protection

Matthew 6:13
*'And lead us not into temptation, **but** deliver us from the evil one.'*

If we try to live as Christ's disciples in our own strength, we are doomed to failure. We need to ask for his help. We need to ask for his protection. And he is a God who **loves** to protect his people!

Do you want to be a genuine disciple? Do you want to be used by God to bring genuine change to this world? It all starts with prayer. Genuine prayer. Can you use this model of prayer to change the way you talk to God? Go on – give it a try! And stand back and watch the results!

4. GENUINE WORSHIP

Jesus wants you to be the best. Jesus is calling you to have genuine worship. Not second-rate worship. Not: *'Hey everyone look at me and see how great I am'* worship.

Genuine worship. Revolutionary worship. He wants you to be the best.

He wants us to be the best givers. The best pray-ers. The best worshippers. He wants his name to be honoured here on earth – through us! This is a call to be genuine. Jesus wants your heart. Later in Matthew's Gospel, Jesus quotes from the prophet Isaiah saying:

'JESUS WANTS YOU TO BE THE BEST'

Matthew 15:8
'These people honour me with their lips, but their hearts are far from me'

'JESUS IS CALLING YOU TO HAVE GENUINE WORSHIP'

Let's avoid being counterfeit disciples where *'it's all about me'*. As genuine disciples, let's come humbly before Jesus and confess: *'it's all about you'*.

'This book has helped me by showing me how to be a genuine disciple. It has challenged me on what it means to be a Christian and what it really involves. It has also reminded me to put God first in everything and he will look after me.'

Jason, Year 6

1. HOW DO YOU WORK OUT WHAT'S REALLY IMPORTANT?

Okay – how **do** you work out what's really important to someone? How do you determine what really matters to them? Is it based on what they **say** – or do you get a better clue from what they **do**?

> There's a dad in a family and he works 14 hours a day, 6 days a week, and when his family grumbles that he's never home, he says: '*But I'm doing it for you guys*'.

What's really important to him?

> There's a girl who spends three hours in front of the mirror before she comes to church – making sure that every hair is exactly in place, and every kilogram of makeup has been plastered on in precisely the right proportions.

What's really important to her?

> There's a guy who's got a new girlfriend, but unfortunately for her, he's also got a new car! Even though he **says** to his girlfriend that she's the most important thing in his life – he spends far more time and money on his new car than he does on his woman!

What's really important to him?

> There's a leader in a youth group who never has enough money to be generous with the offering at church, but owns the absolute latest of every techno-gadget imaginable.

How do you work out what's important to someone?

You can always check out what's really important to someone. There are some absolute dead-set give-aways. Usually it's got nothing to do with what a person **says** is important. You can always find out what's important to any person by checking these three areas:

> How you spend your time.
>
> How you spend your money.
>
> What you worry about.

When you check these three things out, what's **really** important to you will be dead obvious!

2. HOW DO YOU CHECK WHAT'S IMPORTANT IN YOUR CHRISTIAN LIFE?

Exactly the same way.

Because often what a Christian **says** is really important to them is not what's **really** important to them at all. Sometimes what a Christian **says** they're trusting in is not what they're trusting in at all. You'll always be given away by checking out those three areas:

> How you spend your time.
>
> How you spend your money.
>
> What you worry about.

3. MAKING DISCIPLESHIP COUNT

Jesus is teaching us some powerful stuff in this 'Sermon on the Mount'. He's teaching us how to be his genuine disciples. We've seen how he wants us to have genuine success. We've discovered how he wants us to have genuine obedience.

He has revealed to us how we can offer genuine worship. Right now we're going to learn how to develop genuine trust.

In the end, you will always trust the things that actually are the most important things in your life. And we will all know the most important things in your life by checking out three areas:

How you spend your time.
How you spend your money.
What you worry about.

Let's check them out now.

Matthew 6:19-20

'Do not store up for yourselves treasures on earth, where moth and rust destroy, and where thieves break in and steal. But store up for yourselves treasures in heaven, where moth and rust do not destroy, and where thieves do not break in and steal.'

Jesus says there is a clear choice you can make as to where you put your time. You can either put your time and effort into accumulating treasures on earth – or you can put your time and effort into accumulating treasures in heaven. You can focus your efforts on things that have absolutely no value in God's kingdom. But if you're **really** trusting God, you'll make sure you stay focused on achieving great things which are of lasting value in God's kingdom.

4. TREASURES ON EARTH

Matthew 6:19

'Do not store up for yourselves treasures on earth...'

Why not? 'Treasures on earth' can be **so** attractive!

I remember buying my first car. I paid £100 of my hard-earned money, and became the proud owner of a 1959 VW Beetle. This was my pride and joy! In the first few months that I owned it, I hardly stayed home at all. I was always out driving. I cleaned it every week. Polished it. Degreased it. Accessorised it. Painted it. Lavished it with constant attention. This was the most valuable thing I had ever owned!

Getting new stuff is always like that. The new outfit. The new shoes. The new mobile phone. The new iPod. The new computer. All great stuff! All so much fun! All **soooo** desirable. But Jesus says: '*Do not store up for yourselves treasures on earth*'.

Why not? What's the big problem?

5. PROBLEMS ON EARTH

Jesus goes on to give us the main problem of placing your trust in 'treasures on earth'.

Matthew 6:19
'*Do not store up for yourselves treasures on earth, where moth and rust destroy, and where thieves break in and steal.*'

Hmm – that can be a problem – can't it? Doesn't take that long for that car of yours to get a few scratches. A few dings. (*Maybe you've even managed to prang it!*)

That new outfit which is so fashionable – so desirable – so 'in'. Six months later ... it is so out of fashion you wouldn't be seen dead in it!

That new computer that was so 'cutting edge' when you bought it. But now it's so old – so slow – so big – so inadequate – so embarrassing

That new mobile phone ... which had all your friends gawking at it when you bought it – there are now phones which are **sooo** much better. The new ones play all the latest MP3s – or shoot video with sound – take stunning photos – make you a cup of coffee when you're in a hurry – and that 'old' phone of yours is starting to look a little prehistoric.

Or maybe your iPod keeps breaking down. Or your new fashion sunglasses got stolen. Or you accidentally dropped your mobile phone in the toilet. Or your skateboard broke in two. Or your car just keeps rusting away.

Frustrating, isn't it? That new gadget or new fashion item – the satisfaction doesn't last for long. Once it gets broken, damaged, stolen, scratched, worn out, superseded – the happiness doesn't last much time at all!

6. TREASURES IN HEAVEN

Jesus says: *'Don't put all your time and effort into accumulating the goodies that this earth has to offer. They wear out. They break down. They disappoint you. And they never satisfy you – you always want more.'*

He has a better suggestion:

> *'Put your time and effort into the treasures in heaven. These things last for eternity.*
>
> *They never break down. They never get outdated. They will never get taken away from you.'*

Treasures in heaven?

Yeah – you know what some of these are. These are the things that are given to you by God. They last forever. They can't be damaged. And they will **never** be taken away.

Things like: *eternal life... being forgiven by God... growing as God's child... being a genuine disciple... having a ministry to others... helping your friend become a Christian...*

All these are treasures in heaven – they last for eternity – and are more valuable than any price you could pay. Jesus says: *'Put your time and effort there.'*

7. WHAT'S IMPORTANT TO YOU?

Remember our three checkpoints?

How you spend your time.

How you spend your money.

What you worry about.

So – if you want to check how you're going as a disciple, work out how you're spending your time. Storing up treasure on earth? Or storing up treasure in heaven?

That will show what's really important to you. Then you will know where you're really placing your trust. And then you will know what 'the cry of your heart' really is!

16 CHECKPOINT 2 – YOUR MONEY

Matthew 6:21-24

Remember our three checkpoints? The three things that will tell you what really matters to you? The three things that will show you where you're really placing your trust?

How you spend your time.

How you spend your money.

What you worry about.

Okay, let's check out the second one – 'How you spend your money'. There are two reasons why this is vitally important. Here is the first:

1. WHERE IS YOUR HEART?

Matthew 6:21

'For where your treasure is, there your heart will be also.'

Do you want to know whether you have a genuine heart for God? Do you want to know the state of your spiritual heart?

'WHERE YOUR TREASURE IS, THERE YOUR HEART WILL BE ALSO'

You know what happens when someone wants to check out the state of their physical heart. Maybe they're concerned because their heart is not beating regularly. Perhaps they're worried about a pain across their chest. Something is wrong – and they suspect their heart is the problem. How do they check it?

They head off to the doctor, and get rigged up for an 'ECG'. Fancy letters that hide a fancy word – an 'Electrocardiogram'. The doctor will rig up all sorts of wires to the patient's chest, which will record a readout of their actual heartbeat. This all gets printed out on a graph, and then anyone who looks at it can know for sure what is the state of the patient's heart.

Wouldn't it be good if we could rig up some sort of test to check the state of your **spiritual** heart? To know whether your heart was on fire for God? To check whether you had the heart of a true disciple?

Here's the good news! You can always check where your spiritual heart is at. Jesus gives us the clue:

> **Matthew 6:21**
> *'For where your treasure is, there your heart will be also'.*

Wanna know how your heart is going for God? **Simply check where your treasure is!** Whatever you're pouring your dollars into at the moment will show God – and will show everyone who sees you – where your heart really is.

You see it matters to God where your heart is. Remember what Jesus said?

> **Matthew 22:37**
> *'Love the Lord your God with **all your heart** and with all your soul and with all your mind.'*

2. WHO IS YOUR MASTER?

Here is a second question as to why it is so vital to work out how you spend your money.

> **Matthew 6:24**
> *'No one can serve two masters. Either he will hate the one and love the other, or he will be devoted to the one and despise the other.'*

It's not hard to understand that you can't serve two masters.

Imagine playing sport on a team – and your team has two coaches – and they're standing on opposite sides of the field – and they're both shouting out different orders! One coach wants you to run forward – the other coach wants you to hold back! You can't obey them both! You can't serve two masters!

Or maybe you're learning to drive. Imagine you go out with your 'L' plates on – and you've got your dad sitting next to you in the car – and your mum is also in the back seat. **Both** of them start giving you different instructions at the one time! Your dad says to you '*Speed up!*', and at the same time, your mum yells out '*Slow down!*' This is an impossible situation! You can't obey them both! You can't serve two masters!

We can all agree with the principle that 'you can't serve two masters'. But look at the conclusion Jesus draws!

> ### Matthew 6:24
> '*No one can serve two masters. Either he will hate the one and love the other, or he will be devoted to the one and despise the other. **You cannot serve both God and Money**'.*

Jesus is not saying that a Christian can't have money. Perhaps God wants you to have buckets of money so that you can generously give to support God's work!

But here's what really matters – what is ruling you? What is controlling you? What's influencing you to make your decisions? Is your world ruled by God – or is your world ruled by money?

Where you spend your money is a dead give-away as to what really matters to you. And where you spend

'ARE YOU RULED BY GOD – OR ARE YOU RULED BY MONEY'

your money will increasingly show **what is controlling you**. Where you put your money will always show you where your heart is – and it will show you who your true master is.

Think about this:

> *If you are serving money more and more,*
> *then you will give your God away more and more.*
> *But if you are serving God more and more,*

*then you will give your **money** away more and more.*

That's how you show you are not mastered by something. You give it away. **If you can't give it away, it shows you are still mastered by it.**

So – do you really want to know 'the cry of your heart'? Then check out where your treasure is!

'IF YOU CAN'T GIVE IT AWAY, IT SHOWS THAT YOU ARE STILL MASTERED BY IT.'

17 CHECKPOINT 3 – WHAT YOU WORRY ABOUT

Matthew 6:25-30

We've been looking at three things that will tell you what really matters to you. Three things that will show you where you're really placing your trust.

How you spend your time.

How you spend your money.

What you worry about.

On to the last one – 'What you worry about.' Let's check it out. What occupies your mind? What do you get concerned about? What issues do you devote time and effort and money into making sure you solve?

1. WHAT WILL I EAT AND DRINK?

I've worked with teenagers for over thirty years. Some of the greatest people on our planet are teenagers. Some of my best friends are teenagers. So I know how the teenage body works. I know what goes through your mind. Even when you are occupied in reading a book like this, there is a thought that keeps capturing your mind and taking your attention away from the task at hand.

'When do we eat?'

C'mon, you're feeling a bit hungry, aren't you? When can I have a snack? When's the next meal? How can I get to the coke machine?

Jesus might want you to be dreaming about those pearly gates of heaven. But you might simply be dreaming about the golden arches of fast food!

'If only I could have a pizza and coke I'd be satisfied.'

2. WHAT WILL I WEAR?

There is of course a second question that occupies stacks of our time and energy:

> 'What will I wear?'

Now I know this one really matters. You want to look your best. You want to look trendy. You want to look funky. You want to look attractive. You want to look in-fashion. You want to look thin.

And teenagers are some of the snappiest dressers around! And there's nothing wrong with looking good. But have you ever gone on a camp with lots of other teenagers? Maybe just an overnight school camp. Or a church camp that lasts for a weekend. **Have you seen the amount of luggage some people bring?** Some people seem to bring two or three complete new outfits for every day!

A lot of what we worry about is working out what we can eat or drink. A lot of what we worry about is working out what we will wear.

Jesus says:

> **Matthew 6:25**
> *'Therefore I tell you, do not worry about your life, what you will eat or drink; or about your body, what you will wear...'*

All these might be important things, but ... there are a lot more crucial things that God wants you to focus on!

3. LIFE IS MORE THAN THAT!

> **Matthew 6:25**
> *'Therefore I tell you, do not worry about your life, what you will eat or drink; or about your body, what you will wear. Is not life more important than food, and the body more important than clothes?'*

This is the cry of Jesus' heart. This is what he is saying:

> *'There's bigger stuff I want you to focus on. I don't want you to*

spend all your time worrying about what you will eat, what you will drink, what you will wear. I am calling you to be my genuine disciple. I have a world that I want you to go out and change. You have friends at your school that I want to call to myself. I have a lifetime of discipleship and ministry that I am preparing you for. There are nations that are going to be turned to me because of you'.

Give up just worrying about what you're going to eat and what you're going to wear! Let me worry about that! I want you to trust me that I'm going to look after you. I want you to focus on changing your life to be my faithful disciple. I want you to focus on winning this world for me – one life at a time.'

You're saying that you can't give up more time for ministry cos you don't have any time. You're saying that you've got a pressure year of study and you can't spend the time going to your Bible-study group. You're saying that you can't be bothered talking about me to your friends cos they're not going to listen anyway! You think if you put your money in the offering, then you're not going to be able to buy stuff to wear!'

There is one over-arching thing that God wants to say to you.

God is saying to you now: '**Trust me!**'

4. GOD CAN BE TRUSTED

You want to have some solid evidence that God can be trusted?

Matthew 6:26
'Look at the birds of the air; they do not sow or reap or store away in barns, and yet your heavenly Father feeds them. Are you not much more valuable than they?'

Go out any day. Look at the birds flying around. Seagulls hovering over you at the beach. Pigeons landing in the park. Who looks after them?

Jesus makes the point – *'Birds don't 'go to work' as we do. They don't plant*

'GOD IS SAYING TO YOU: 'TRUST ME!'

crops. They don't run farms. They don't shop in supermarkets. They don't own credit cards. **And yet God feeds them every day!'**

Jesus' point? '*If God can be trusted to look after the birds, and you are far more valuable than birds are –* **surely you can trust God to look after you!'**

Matthew 6:28-30
'*And why do you worry about clothes? See how the lilies of the field grow. They do not labour or spin. Yet I tell you that not even Solomon in all his splendour was dressed like one of these. If that is how God clothes the grass of the field, which is here today and tomorrow is thrown into the fire, will he not much more clothe you, O you of little faith?'*

Same deal. Go check out the flowers some day. Any flowers will do. Flowers growing in a garden in the park; wildflowers growing out in the countryside. Ask this question – '*What work do the flowers do?'* Yeah – I know – they produce pollen, which is picked up by the bees, to ensure that more and more flowers keep growing – but do they go to work in a factory? Do they operate machinery? Do they produce fabric and clothing? Do they go shopping at the markets for the latest fashions?

No! **But God clothes them magnificently!** In fantastic colours! Even more glorious than the mighty King Solomon!

Jesus' point? '*If God goes to all this effort to clothe the flowers and the grass of the field – which are only here for a day or two before they're plucked out of the ground, or just left to wither and die – how much more can God be trusted to clothe you?'*

Jesus is not against us working hard. He is not opposed to us saving wisely and buying our necessities. But he wants to challenge you: '*What are you really trusting? What's controlling your life?* **Will you trust God to look after you** *– or do you trust him so little that you feel you've gotta do everything yourself?'*

And to back up his challenge, he has one more point to make...

5. WORRYING GETS YOU NOWHERE!

Matthew 6:27
'*Who of you by worrying can add a single hour to his life?'*

When I was a boy, I used to worry about whether I would ever grow tall and become a man. I would stand in front of the mirror and check whether any hairs were ever going to grow on my chest! I wanted to have bigger muscles. I wanted to be six feet tall!

Well yes, I grew to be a man, but I never made it to 6 feet tall! Now, what can I do about this? Can I worry about it? (some teenagers do!) Will worrying about it add one centimetre to my height? Will worrying about my life make me live longer? In fact, does worrying about something ever produce a positive result?

'WORRYING GETS YOU NOWHERE'

One great reason for trusting God is that worrying about something yourself **never achieves anything!**

So – what's the alternative to worrying about things yourself? Next chapter, please!

18 A WHOLE NEW WAY TO TRUST

Matthew 6:31-34

1. LET SOMEONE ELSE DO THE WORRYING!

Matthew 6:31-32

'So do not worry, saying, 'What shall we eat?' or 'What shall we drink?' or 'What shall we wear?' For the pagans run after all these things, and your heavenly Father knows that you need them.'

There's no need to race around worrying *'What shall we eat? What shall we drink? What shall we wear?'* That's why we have shopping centres! An instant supply of everything you could possibly want to eat, drink or wear!

Try this as an experiment. Go down to your local shopping centre, and in your mind, take away all the shops that provide stuff to eat and drink, and then take away all the shops that provide stuff to wear. There aren't many shops left, are there?

Disciples are not meant to have to worry about these things! Jesus says: *'For the pagans run after all these things'*. This is what the **non-Christians** are meant to worry about. This is stuff for the people who don't trust God!

Does that make sense? If you don't have Jesus in your life, there's not a lot of point to life anyway. If you don't have Jesus running your life, there's no real point to life – it just churns away, day in, day out.

You go to work...
to earn the money...
to buy the food...
to get the energy...
to go to work...
to earn the money... and so it goes on...

If you're not sold out on being a genuine disciple ... there's not a lot of point to life. And if you're not sure what you're doing on this planet, you may as well just make sure that you're well-fed and well-dressed. A life without God is just like that. You make yourself as comfortable as possible while you wait to die.

'A LIFE WITHOUT GOD? YOU MAKE YOURSELF AS COMFORTABLE AS POSSIBLE WHILE YOU WAIT TO DIE'

Wouldn't that be terrible if that's all there was to your life?

2. GOD KNOWS WHAT YOU NEED

But that's not for you! God has called you to something different from that. God has called you to something bigger than that. He has given you a real purpose for your life. He has a mission for you to accomplish. He has miracles he wants to do in your own life. And there is a world that he wants you to change for him.

Here's why you do not have to worry about your life. Here's why you can trust God for everything. Here's why you can have genuine peace as you seek to be a genuine disciple:

> **Matthew 6:31-32**
> *'So do not worry, saying, 'What shall we eat?' or 'What shall we drink?' or 'What shall we wear?' For the pagans run after all these things, and **your heavenly Father knows that you need them**.'*

Have you got that? **God already knows what you need!**

Right now – if you need strengthening for your faith – God knows that already. Right now – if you need guidance for the future – God knows that already. Right now – if you need healing from something that is striking you down – if you need your parents to understand you – if you need forgiveness for something stupid that you've done – God knows that already!

You don't have to stress! You don't have to worry! God certainly wants to hear from you – **but he already knows what you need!** You can trust him!

But how do I do that?

There is one verse in the Bible that will show you how. One verse that will get your life in perspective. It will help you make wise decisions as to how you spend your time. It will help you as you face major exams this year. It will stop you from stuffing around putting time and effort and money into things which simply don't matter. You can take this one verse and make it 'the cry of your heart'.

'GOD ALREADY KNOWS WHAT YOU NEED.'

3. PUT GOD FIRST, AND...

Matthew 6:33
'But seek first his kingdom and his righteousness, and all these things will be given to you as well.'

There are two halves to this verse. The first half is the obvious bit – the second half is the surprise.

The clue to being a genuine disciple is to put God first in **everything that you do!** Always! In every situation. Not putting him in second place – not putting him as an added-on extra – not keeping him in your back pocket in case of an emergency. The way to show genuine trust in our great God is to put him first **in everything.**

Now – here's the fun bit – **look what happens when you put God first!** Let's check the verse again:

Matthew 6:33
'But seek first his kingdom and his righteousness, and all these things will be given to you as well.'

Have you got it?

When you put the things of God first in your life – when you put the things of God's kingdom as your main priority – **all the other things in your life fall into the right place!**

And if you **don't** put the things of God first in your life – if you don't put the things of God's kingdom as your main priority – **all these other things will be in the wrong place.**

113

Because when you don't put God in his proper place (first!), **then everything else is out of place!** So if you're having problems with some of the 'everything else's' in your life, work on putting God and his kingdom first, and you'll discover that *'all these things will be given to you as well.'*

I suspect that one of the reasons we sometimes don't trust God – one of the reasons that we don't put him in first place – is that we're scared that if we do, we'll miss out on the things that the world has to offer.

'WHEN YOU TRUST JESUS, YOU DON'T MISS OUT ON ANYTHING THAT'S GOOD FOR YOU'

Trusting God simply means this: If we do what he says – put him first in everything – then that means we leave it to him to sort out all the other stuff. And when you're truly trusting Jesus, **you're not going to miss out on anything that will be good for you!**

4. SO, WHAT WOULD IT LOOK LIKE?

What would it look like if you showed this genuine trust in God? What would it look like if you were part of a church, youth group or Bible-study group where **everybody** took Jesus seriously and put God's kingdom first – and we let God worry about the details of supplying what we needed to get us there?

What **would** it look like?

We would be passionate about prayer – we would be generous in our giving – we would have so many of our friends coming to our church youth group that we wouldn't know what to do with them. Our Bible studies would keep running over time cos we'd be so concerned to know God better. We wouldn't be able to fit everyone in at church. We would live in a community of disciples that puts God and his kingdom first in **everything.** We would be part of a body of believers who offer to God **genuine trust.**

What would it mean for you personally?

You would be a faithful disciple putting God's kingdom first and trusting God with your whole life. You would be confident knowing that God was looking after you and guiding you every step of the way. You'd be leaving aside the sin that is dragging you down right now, because you would trust God to give you the strength to deal with it. You would joyfully submit to your parents and honour Christ in your household. You would know that your heart was right.

Wouldn't you love to be like that? Is there something in your life that is keeping God out of first place? Is there an issue facing you right now where you're struggling to trust God? Is there a relationship that you're in – or something that you own – or something that you want – or something that you're doing – that is starting to control your thoughts and dominate your life?

'SEEK FIRST GOD'S KINGDOM' – THAT'S THE CRY OF MY HEART!'

Where do you need to make a change? Are you game to make that change now so that you can start enjoying the faith-filled life of a disciple? Can you look at this verse and honestly say: '*That's the cry of my heart!*'?

Matthew 6:33
'*But seek first his kingdom and his righteousness, and all these things will be given to you as well.*'

'Thank you for writing what is real! I realised through this book that being a genuine disciple is so much more than just doing 'the Christian stuff''.

Ashleigh, Year 12

5 GENUINE DANGERS

19 DANGER 1 – JUDGING OTHERS

Matthew 7:1-6

1. DANGERS

There are dangers everywhere in life. Things that could go wrong. Places where you could get hurt. Dangerous detours which could take you away from where you're meant to be. Side-tracks that take you away from safety.

Sometimes these dangers are obvious. But sometimes we need someone else to point them out to us.

> Little kids aren't aware of the many dangers that lie around them. When you were a little kid, you would have happily played out on the busy road. If mum or dad hadn't dragged you back and warned you about it, you would have been in a place of real danger. If you ever saw pretty sparks coming out of the old toaster – you needed someone else to point out the danger to you!

There are dangers everywhere!

> When I was a teenager, I went surfing at one of the many surf beaches in Sydney. I wasn't a great swimmer, but as long as I wasn't out of my depth, I was fine. But there was a danger I was unaware of. I thought I was safe in the water, but I was standing on a sand-bar. When the sand-bar eventually collapsed, I was in deep trouble! I needed to be rescued by a lifeguard!

There are dangers everywhere. If you play sport, you run the risk of breaking a bone. If you ride your bike, you run the risk of falling off and grazing your skin. If you're in the woods and you take refuge in a gingerbread cottage, you run the risk of being captured by a wicked witch.

Indeed – if you're a typical teenager – one of the most dangerous places in the world is your own bedroom! Old dirty clothes lie on top of clean clothes on your floor – and who knows what bacteria are breeding there! Decomposing food scraps have been accidentally left under your bed – producing a weird smell that no one can identify. Anything you leave lying around in your room has the danger of disappearing into a black vortex and never being able to be found again!

There are dangers everywhere!

2. WARNINGS

Now some of the really nifty things in this world are 'warnings'. Yeah, yeah – I know – you **hate** warnings – but if you look at it carefully, they're kinda useful.

One day you and your friends decide to go exploring in the electrical substation which is down the road. You pass a sign that says: '*Danger – 250,000 volts*'. Now, this probably slows you down a bit on your illegal exploration – but the warning is a good thing. It's alerting you to a danger. It's actually there to save your life.

Imagine you're driving your first car along some country road. There's a warning sign which says: '*Danger – Sharp Bend*'. But you hate obeying warnings, so you forge on ahead regardless. You make it around the corner at high speed, and by now you're feeling invincible. The next sign says: '*Danger – Roadworks Ahead*' – but who cares? You step on the accelerator and manage to swerve around the repair gang on the road. The third warning sign says: '*Danger – Stop – Bridge Out – No way through*'. Now, I know you don't like warnings, and you've managed to survive even though you've ignored the last two signs, but are you starting to think 'I should obey this one'? Warning signs might feel like a nuisance, but they're there to warn you of danger and protect you.

3. DANGERS FOR DISCIPLES

There are many dangers for anyone who is striving to live as a genuine disciple. All sorts of sidetracks which will take you away from following Jesus. Really powerful temptations that are designed to make you less effective in the world for Jesus.

And God cares enough about your journey of faith to warn you where the danger spots are. So if you want to continue strongly as a genuine disciple, Matthew chapter 7 spells out five dangers that you will need to avoid. Five warning signs so that you will not fall into difficulties.

These dangers are real. The warning signs matter. So if you want to power on as a genuine disciple – pay attention!

4. DON'T JUDGE OTHERS

One of the real dangers in reading a book like this – or in listening to Jesus' words from 'The Sermon on the Mount' – is to immediately see where **everyone else** is getting it wrong! I don't think I like admitting when I've made a mistake, and it can be kinda easy to just criticise and judge others. This is the first danger that Jesus wants to warn us about.

Matthew 7:1

'Do not judge...'

Yeah? Why not? Why can't I have a good whinge about how badly everyone else treats me?

Jesus gives two reasons:

a) You might be judged the same way!

Matthew 7:1-2

'Do not judge, or you too will be judged. For in the same way you judge others, you will be judged, and with the measure you use, it will be measured to you'.

O my goodness! Can you imagine other people judging and criticising you the same way that you judge and criticise them? Or here's a worse thought – can you imagine **God** judging and criticising you the same way that you judge and criticise others?

Ouch! Imagine if God was as unforgiving as you are! Or imagine that God complained as much as you do! Imagine that God was as critical as you are! Here's the principle – if you want God to be accepting and forgiving of you, then you need to model this in how you treat others.

IMAGINE IF GOD COMPLAINED AS MUCH AS YOU DO!

The same thought is there when Jesus teaches us how to pray:

Matthew 6:12

'Forgive us our debts, as we also have forgiven our debtors.'

The rest of the Bible backs this up.

Romans 15:7

'Accept one another, then, just as Christ accepted you'

So – there's a good reason not to be judgmental of others. Think about the way you judge and criticise others and ask yourself this question – *'Would I like to be treated this way by God – or by others?'*

The principle that Jesus will keep going back to is this:

Matthew 7:12

'So in everything, do to others what you would have them do to you...'

But there's a second reason why Jesus doesn't want us to fall into the trap of judging others:

b)   Fix up your own act first!

Matthew 7:3-5

'Why do you look at the speck of sawdust in your brother's eye and pay no attention to the plank in your own eye? How can you say to your brother, 'Let me take the speck out of your eye,' when all the time there is a plank in your own eye? You hypocrite, first take the plank out of your own eye, and then you will see clearly to remove the speck from your brother's eye.'

This is an absolutely outrageous, ridiculous story. Try and picture this: your friend is walking along the road, and you can see that there is a tiny speck in his eye. He seems unaware of it – but you can see it clearly. He looks such a scruff with this speck in his eye! You wonder why he doesn't do anything about it! I mean, how can someone be so sloppy and lazy as to walk along the street with such a facial deformity!

'JESUS TEACHING IS CLEAR: FIRST FIX UP YOUR OWN MESS'

You feel the need to criticise him. You feel the need to fix this problem for him. But just before you race up and start condemning him for his slovenly appearance, Jesus says: *'Hang on! You're getting upset about this tiny speck in your brother's eye – you're so quick to condemn him for something so small – and yet you're ignoring a much bigger problem that you have yourself!'*

Jesus goes on to describe your own problem that you're totally ignoring. He talks about you walking around with a great plank sticking out from your eye! Imagine that! It's a ridiculous scene! You're parading about with a huge bit of timber sticking out from your face – bumping into people – knocking them over – being a hazard to everyone who comes across you.

Do you see the point that Jesus is making? It's so easy to see even the tiny faults that other people have, but be blind to your own failings. The reason that Jesus is teaching us this stuff – is not so we can go around and criticise others. Jesus wants us to face our own issues – and fix up the things that are stopping us from being genuine disciples.

I need to take this to heart myself. Is there a plank in my own eye that I'm ignoring? Is there something about my walk as a disciple that needs fixing up? Jesus' teaching is clear: first fix up your own mess. Then you may be of some value in helping someone else with their mess.

5. BUT BE CAREFUL

Now don't take Jesus the wrong way. He's not saying we can **never** make an assessment about how someone else is going. We're not meant to keep trusting every single person in the world – when perhaps the other person is demonstrating that they are not worthy of our trust.

Matthew 7:6

*'Do not give dogs what is sacred; do not throw your pearls to pigs. If you
do, they may trample them under their feet, and then turn and tear you
to pieces.'*

It's a simple principle: if you have something incredibly valuable, don't just
give it to people who will destroy it. If you have a mobile phone, you don't
throw it to your dog to play with. It'll get destroyed! If you're on a farm, you
don't take your prize jewellery and offer it to your pigs! They'll trample it under
their feet – and then maybe even turn on you!

So while Jesus is saying: *'Don't judge other people'*, he is also saying: *'Be wise in
how much you trust them'*. If people keep trashing your stuff, don't keep giving
it to them. There comes a point where you will only be able to help people
when they want your help.

**'THE HEART OF A DISCIPLE IS
TO DEAL WITH YOUR OWN SIN'**

There is Danger 1 –
Judging others. Be on your
guard so that you don't
just end up critical and
complaining of other people. This sort of attitude will take you away from
being a genuine disciple. The heart of a disciple is to deal with your own sin,
rather than judging everyone else's.

20 DANGER 2 — NOT TRUSTING GOD

Matthew 7:7-12

1. SOMETIMES IT'S HARD TO TRUST

I think it's hard to trust others. You've probably had some bad experiences when you placed your trust in someone else. Maybe you've been let down. Badly.

> Ian was a teenager whom I knew years ago. He was from a troubled background. He had been taken away from his parents at an early age – he had been brought up in foster homes – and during his teenage years he had been in and out of trouble with the law. He had been in a juvenile prison – but had now turned 18, and he had nowhere to go.
>
> I let him stay with me. I was helping him to get on his feet, find a job, and make a go of his life. It *looked* like it was going okay. But one day I came home from work – found that Ian had cleared out – and had stolen some money and other valuables from my house.
>
> I had trusted him. He had betrayed me. I felt let down. And I probably would be more careful with who I trusted next time.

Maybe people you have trusted have let you down as well. That best friend who turned against you and spread those lies about you. That boyfriend or girlfriend who *said* they would always be loyal to you, but they ended up dumping you and going out with one of your friends. Maybe your mum or dad promised you something but never followed through. You might have even been hurt or abused by someone who broke your trust.

Sometimes, it can be really hard to trust others. People will let you down. People will hurt you. It can seem as if it's just not worth trusting anyone anymore.

2. SOMETIMES IT'S HARD TO TRUST GOD

Maybe it even feels as if God has let you down. Perhaps you were desperately praying for something, but God didn't give you the answer you were looking for. Maybe someone who was close to you was sick – and you were fervently praying for their healing – but they never recovered. Maybe someone was hurting you and you prayed to God that it would stop – and it didn't. Maybe you really wanted God to be there for you, but it felt as if you had been left alone.

'SOMETIMES IT'S HARD TO TRUST GOD'

Even though you know that God is there for you, sometimes it can feel as if he's left you.

God understands that we feel like that. He knows when we're hurting. He knows when we need him. And he knows that we sometimes doubt him.

And one of the dangers for a disciple is that they will give in to their feelings and give up trusting God. Jesus wants to warn us of that danger – and he wants to show us – in clear and simple terms – **no matter what it feels like, God will never let us down.**

3. CAN YOU TRUST GOD AS A 'DAD'?

Matthew 7:9-11
> *'Which of you, if his son asks for bread, will give him a stone? Or if he asks for a fish, will give him a snake? If you, then, though you are evil, know how to give good gifts to your children, how much more will your Father in heaven give good gifts to those who ask him!'*

Imagine there's a little boy – and he's hungry – he hasn't eaten for ages, and he's starting to feel a bit weak. He's standing next to his dad, and so he turns to him and asks him for a piece of bread. Or maybe a piece of fish.

What's the dad going to do? Even the worst dad in the world knows how to feed his kids. Jesus asks this question in the passage: *'If your kid is hungry, and asks for a piece of bread – is there a dad anywhere who would hand him a rock and say 'Here – munch on this!' Of course not! Or if your starving son asks for a piece of fish, what dad in the world would serve him a poisonous snake that might jump out and kill him?'*

I don't know what sort of a dad you've got. Maybe you've got the best dad in the world – or the worst dad in the world. Every dad in the world makes mistakes.

They all stuff things up. Sometimes they don't act in the best interests of their children. Sometimes they are selfish and harsh in dealing with their kids.

But **usually** they do the right thing by us. And when it gets down to providing us with the basic stuff of life, most dads know how to do it. And the fact that the human race has survived up to this point shows that dads more-or-less know how to provide for their kids.

But look at the point that Jesus makes about God being our perfect heavenly Dad:

4. GOD WANTS TO SAY 'YES' TO YOU

Matthew 7:11
'If you, then, though you are evil, know how to give good gifts to your children, how much more will your Father in heaven give good gifts to those who ask him!'

Jesus makes this point – if our own dads (who are imperfect) know how to give good things to their kids, how much more does God – our perfect heavenly Dad – know how to give us good things – always!

God is just waiting to hear from you because there are good things he wants to shower you with! Can you imagine that! God is like the dad who just wants to give you stacks and stacks of things which will be good for you.

He's on your side. He's there for you.

Is that your picture of God – that he loves to say 'yes' to you? Do you trust him enough that you will bring every request to him because you know he loves to say 'yes'?

Or do you see God as someone who loves to say 'no'? You know – a mean old grouch, who hates to see us enjoying ourselves and loves to watch us suffer. Do you imagine that God is like the cranky old man who lives down the street and yells at you every time you ride your skateboard down the road, and won't give you your ball back when you accidentally kick it into his garden?

'Dear God – can you please get me a boyfriend (or girlfriend) ?' **'No!'**

'Dear God – will you help me?' **'No!'**

'Dear God – can I please have some fun?' **'No!'**

Do you picture God like that? A God who loves to say 'no!'? Do you imagine that God is there waiting to stop you from doing something enjoyable? That he just sits there all day dreaming up more commandments that start with the words *'Thou shalt not'*?

'Look God, there are some people down on earth having fun!'

'Don't worry – I'll make up a commandment that will stop that!'

No! No! No! God is nothing like that. Remember – Jesus says:

Matthew 7:11
' how much more will your Father in heaven give good gifts to those who ask him!'

Do you want good things in your life? **Then ask God!** God is there **wanting** to give you good things! **Wanting** to shower you with blessings. **Wanting** to give you everything you need so you can power ahead as his genuine disciple!

You mean all I've gotta do is ask? **Yes!**

But how do I do that?

5. GOD WANTS TO HEAR FROM YOU – NOW!

God absolutely wants the best for you. He wants to hear from you. He wants you to come to him and do three things: ask, seek and knock.

Let's check them out one by one.

a) Ask

Matthew 7:7-8

'Ask and it will be given to you; seek and you will find; knock and the door
will be opened to you. For everyone who asks receives; he who seeks finds;
and to him who knocks, the door will be opened.'

Because God wants to give you good things, he wants you to **ask** for them.
And if you're asking for something that will be good for you, then the promise
from verse 7 is clear: *'Ask and it will be given to you.'*

> When I was in Bible college, I used my VW Kombi to transport my
> youth group around. One day the engine seized, and it would have
> cost me over £300 to fix it. This was approximately £300 more than I
> had! But I believed God wanted me to get it fixed because I was using
> it to help so many kids. I prayed for the money – and in the next few
> weeks, from about four different sources, just over £300 arrived for
> me. God answered my prayer – and my Kombi was fixed!

> When my wife and I were looking to buy a home, there was no
> way that we had enough money for one. We prayed to God,
> and a builder in our congregation wanted to support our
> ministry – so he offered to build us a house **at cost price**.
> He sold us the house for £40,000 **less** than the market
> value. God answered our prayer – and we moved into our
> new house.

God has promised he will give us **good things** when we ask
for them. Of course, God will answer in **his way** – in his
time – which might not always be what we had in mind.
And of course, if we're praying for something that
God knows will be **bad** for us, then we might find we
don't get it.

Is there something good that you need to help
you live as a genuine disciple? Do you trust God
enough that he will give you the answer that he knows
is best? Then **ask him!**

Well, go on! Do it!

b) Seek

Matthew 7:7b
'Seek and you will find...'

I am one of the worst people at finding things. If something is lost, I have no idea of where to look for it. I lose my keys. I don't know where they are. When I start looking, I tend to **think** I will never find them. And when I think I will never find them, I tend to give up easily.

Do you give up easily when you're asking for things from God?
Do you believe his promise that if you're honestly seeking – you will find?

And do you know the main thing you will find if you honestly seek? **God himself!**

Everyone throughout the world thinks that God is hard to find. They work out all sorts of complicated religions with intricate rituals so that people might have a chance of finding God.

But here is what God says:

Jeremiah 29:11-14
*' For I know the plans I have for you' declares the Lord 'plans to prosper you and not to harm you, plans to give you hope and a future. Then you will call upon me and come and pray to me, and I will listen to you. **You will seek me and find me when you seek me with all your heart. I will be found by you.**'*

Sometimes you can be looking for all sorts of things in your life, when what you're meant to be looking for is God himself.

c) Knock

Matthew 7:7c
'Knock and the door will be opened to you.'

Do you want to know the way forward? Do you want to see some specific answers? Do you want to meet with God himself? Knock and the door will be opened!

Now, there are different sorts of knocking:

You're in trouble at school. You've been sent to the principal's office.

As you approach his door, you're **desperately** hoping that he's not there. You know that if you knock, and there's no reply, then you won't have to face him that day.

So you knock – *really softly* – desperately hoping he won't answer. After one little tap – you hear no reply – you breathe a sigh of relief – and run away as fast as you can!

Is that the way you pray to God? One little prayer – you're assuming he won't hear you – and if you don't get an instant reply, you scurry away and never bother him again?

Or is it more like this?

You're knocking on your girlfriend's door – you desperately want to see her, you know she's home, and you've bought her a bunch of flowers. You knock on her door. No answer. You knock harder. Still no reply. You go around the back and knock on the back door. You tap on every window. You call out. You know she's there and you're not leaving until she answers!

That's the way God wants you to 'knock'. **That's** the way God wants you to pray. He wants you to genuinely seek him – because he is longing to shower you with good gifts.

Trusting God. It's so important. Because if you don't trust him, you won't ask him. And if you don't ask him, you won't get what you need to keep powering on as his genuine disciple.

That's Danger 2 – Not trusting God.

21 DANGER 3 — JUST TAKING THE EASY WAY

Matthew 7:13-14

1. LOOKING FOR THE EASY WAY

I love all our modern inventions. It's great to have so many machines and gadgets that make life easier. We've got machines that transport us across the countryside, wash our clothes, mow our lawns, entertain us, enable us to access information, help us stay in touch, play whatever music we want, fly like the birds...

If our great-great-grandparents could see all the labour-saving gadgets that we possess – they

'YOU DON'T CHOOSE A ROAD BECAUSE IT LOOKS EASY'

wouldn't know what had hit them! Life is so much easier than it used to be!

And I'm all in favour of making life easier. If there's two ways of doing things, and one way is easier than the other, then why not pick it?

2. SOMETIMES THE EASIEST WAY ISN'T ALWAYS THE BEST

For many years I have coached football. It's always interesting to see what happens at training. I usually have all sorts of training activities up my sleeve – all sorts of drills and exercises that will help improve skills and make them better players.

But do you know what the one thing is that all the guys want to do every time we train? No matter how much work I have put into preparing their practice sessions – no matter how stimulating and creative my exercises and activities are, there is one activity that the guys **always** want to do – **they want to play a game!**

Why? Playing a game is always more fun than just doing a training exercise!

Now, think about this. Tell me which of the following two exercises makes it **easier** to score a goal:

a) Standing around an open goal having shot after shot at training.

b) Trying to score a goal in a game against an opposition.

I suspect the answer is a). Far easier to score a goal if you're standing around an open goal – with no one standing in your way – with an endless supply of balls – and loads of time to practise and practise. Scoring goals in a game is much harder – you have limited opportunities, far fewer chances, and there's a hefty fullback and an energetic goalkeeper trying to block you every time!

No doubt as to which one is easier. But here's the real question – **which one is more fun?**

Give the guys a choice any day, and they will **always** pick 'playing a game' as more fun. Can you see – the easiest option is not always the best?

Imagine you're out with a group of friends one afternoon, and you all decide to go for a walk. You have two choices:

a) To walk along the side of the motorway.

b) To follow a winding mountain track.

Which way is easier? Probably a). The motorway is straight, and smooth – there are no huge hills to climb – whereas the mountain track is narrow, difficult, winding, and **all those hills!**

No doubt as to which one is easier. But here's the real question – **which one is more fun?**

I suspect that if you and your friends want to go for a walk together, you will usually pick the mountain track as more fun! Can you see – the easiest option is not always the best?

3. MAKING CHOICES AS A DISCIPLE

You have stacks of choices to make as a disciple. So many times, you will need to make bold decisions as to the best way forward. There's nothing wrong with choosing a way that looks easier, but if your **only** guide for life is *'which way is easiest?'* – you might not always pick the way that is best. Searching for the easy option each time might take you away from Jesus.

Jesus describes that moving forward in life is like making a choice. A choice between two gates. A choice between two roads. A choice between two destinations.

Listen in as Jesus teaches us about making decisions as disciples:

Matthew 7:13-14
'Enter through the narrow gate. For wide is the gate and broad is the road that leads to destruction, and many enter through it. But small is the gate and narrow the road that leads to life, and only a few find it.'

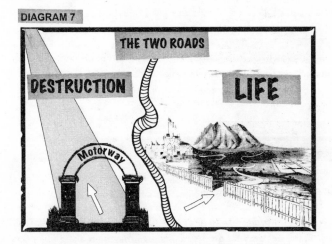

DIAGRAM 7

THE TWO ROADS

DESTRUCTION

LIFE

Motorway

4. THERE ARE TWO ROADS TO CHOOSE

Jesus paints the picture of two gates that we can choose between. The first gate is like a big, wide motorway entrance. Easy to find, hard to miss. The second gate – well, it's kinda small and if you're not looking carefully, you might easily miss it.

From these two gates, there are two roads that head off into the distance. From the wide gate, there is a straight, wide, easy road – like a brand new motorway that heads straight towards the horizon. Lots of people are travelling this way. And from the narrow gate, there is a narrow, winding, difficult path which not many people would choose to travel on.

'YOU CHOOSE A ROAD BECAUSE IT TAKES YOU TO THE RIGHT DESTINATION'

Jesus is not telling us this story so we'll know how to choose roads when we're out driving. Jesus tells us this story **so we'll know how to make decisions as disciples.**

There are lots of people who just take the easier road. This is the *'Do what I want'* road. It looks easier. You don't have to worry about God. You don't have to be concerned with obeying those commandments. You don't have to bother about following Jesus. You can just *'do what you want'*. Lots of people make this choice, because it looks easier.

But the other road – the narrow road – doesn't have many people travelling on it. This is the *'Do what Jesus wants'* road. It **looks** harder. Believing in God. Going to church. Saying your prayers. Being nice to others. A lot of people look at this choice and conclude: *'It looks too hard. I don't think I'd enjoy it'*.

5. EACH ROAD HAS A DESTINATION

But you don't just choose a road based on what looks the easiest. **You choose a road because it takes you to the destination that you want.**

Let's imagine that you want to have a day out at the beach. In my city of Sydney, all the beaches are on the east coast. Imagine making this decision: *'I've found a great road to travel on! There's a brand new motorway! It's better than any other road!'* But imagine how foolish it would be to choose this great new road **if it didn't take you anywhere near the beach!** If the road leads you west – away from the beach – it doesn't matter how good it looks: **If it won't take you to your destination – don't travel on it!**

Jesus says that each of these two roads that he has described has a destination. Jesus says the easy road leads to destruction. And the harder road leads to life.

There are two important things we can learn from this story about making any decision:

a) Don't just do something because it's the easiest way. Do it because it's the **best** way.

b) Don't choose something because it **looks** the easiest. Choose it because it takes you to the destination where you want to go.

6. YOU'RE ACTUALLY IN THIS PICTURE

Did you notice that **you** are actually in this picture of the two roads? These two roads are meant to suggest a decision that **everyone** has to make at some stage. The whole of humanity is travelling on one road or the other. And you're there as well.

Where are you? Go back to the picture on page 133 and work out where you are. Right now. Which way are you travelling?

Are you standing in front of the two gates – trying to make your choice? You need to make your choice. You can't stay undecided for long. Or maybe you've just started on one road – or the other. Or maybe you're a long way down one road – or the other. Perhaps you thought you were travelling on Jesus' road – but as you've read this book, you might have worked out that you were only pretending.

Where are you? It's your choice. Nobody else can change it for you.

But here's the important thing you've got to work out. Wherever you have placed yourself on the two roads, **where is it leading you?** And are you happy with where it will take you?

One way will take you back to Jesus – and life. The other way will take you right away from Jesus – and closer to destruction.

So what road are you on – **and are you happy with where it will take you?**

7. IF YOU WANTED TO CHANGE

If you realise that you are in fact heading away from Jesus – and you want to come back – how can you do that? Let me share with you what Matthew records about Jesus later in his Gospel. Three years after Jesus spoke these words in his 'Sermon on the Mount' – after his enemies had led him out to his death – look carefully at what Jesus went through **so you can come back.**

Jesus has been hanging on the cross all day. He is near the end of his life. This is what Matthew records:

> **Matthew 27:45-46**
> *'From the sixth hour until the ninth hour darkness came over all the land. About the ninth hour Jesus cried out in a loud voice ... 'My God, my God, why have you abandoned me?'*

'ALL YOU'VE GOT TO DO IS COME BACK TO JESUS'

Right there – on the cross – Jesus is all alone. He is dying to take the sins of the world upon himself. He is dying to take **your** sin. And because he is covered in sin – our sin – God his Father turns away from him, as God cannot stand sin in his presence. Jesus is suffering being abandoned by God. That's what hell is. Being locked out of God's presence. On the cross, Jesus takes your sin – Jesus takes your punishment – Jesus takes your hell – so that you can be forgiven and offered the gift of eternal life. By his death on the cross, Jesus makes it possible for you to change sides and come back to him.

But Jesus is not dying as a helpless victim. This is not his moment of defeat! This is his moment of victory! He is the Son of God! He is the Lord of life! God will not abandon him to the grave. On the third day, Jesus will rise as the conqueror of death and the victor over sin.

Look at what happened at the moment that Jesus died:

> **Matthew 27:50-54**
> *'And when Jesus had cried out again in a loud voice, he gave up his spirit. At that moment the curtain of the temple was torn in two from top to bottom. The earth shook and the rocks split. The tombs broke open and the bodies of many holy people who had died were raised to life. They came out of the tombs, and after Jesus' resurrection they went into the*

holy city and appeared to many people. When the centurion and those with him who were guarding Jesus saw the earthquake and all that had happened, they were terrified, and exclaimed, 'Surely he was the Son of God!''

Can you imagine that? Can you picture all those supernatural events happening at the moment that Jesus died? **And he did it all for you!** So that your sins can be taken away! So that you can be forgiven! So that you can live forever with God in heaven!

So how do I make the change?

Matthew also records these words from Jesus:

Matthew 11:28

'Come to me, all you who are weary and burdened, and I will give you rest.'

All you've got to do is to come back to Jesus. And mean it. Mean it now, mean it tomorrow, and mean it for eternity. He is ready and waiting to forgive you. And love you. And place you on that road that will lead you to eternal life.

Talk to him now. Declare to him 'the cry of your heart'. Give your life to him. And tell a trusted Christian friend so that they can help you to **keep going** for Jesus.

That's Danger 3 – Just taking the easy way.

1. HOW DO YOU SPOT THE GENUINE ARTICLE?

Jesus' message in 'The Sermon on the Mount' is all about being genuine. This whole book is designed to help you be a genuine disciple. I'm sure that's what you want to be. I'm sure that's the genuine cry of your heart.

But how do you spot it when **someone else** is not being genuine? When someone else is not the real deal? How do you deal with it when someone is meant to be helping you – guiding you, teaching you – but deep down they're steering you in the wrong direction? What if there's someone who is **asking** for your trust, but maybe they're not **worthy** of your trust?

You might have had some bad experiences here. Maybe you've had a youth leader at your church who has given up on Jesus and walked away. Perhaps your mum or dad has let you down big-time. Or someone has taught you stuff from the Bible which you've later found out is simply not true.

> My childhood was a bit like that. When I started school, I was sent to the local church school. I was taught by a series of nuns, and I'm sure many of them were good and kind people. But when I think back to what they taught me about God, I don't think they got it right. They taught me that I had to do good things to make myself good enough for God. They gave me the impression that if I went to church, said my prayers, and kept all the commandments, that I would be okay. As long as a priest got to me just before I died, all my sins could be forgiven. And that I might have to suffer in a place called 'purgatory' before I could be pure enough to enter heaven. I was 18 years old before I discovered that the Bible said something **completely different!**

So – how would you work it out if somebody was teaching you the wrong things about the Bible? How would you work out whether a church leader was genuinely trying to help you, or whether they were just in it for themselves? If you're going to be a disciple who is genuine, how do you spot the teacher who is fake?

2. WHAT A FALSE TEACHER LOOKS LIKE

Matthew 7:15
'Watch out for false prophets. They come to you in sheep's clothing, but inwardly they are ferocious wolves.'

In Jesus' time, there were false religious leaders. There were people who **sounded** like they were teaching you the Bible, but who were really trying to convince other people with their **own ideas**. Things haven't changed that much in twenty one centuries! There are still stacks of people around who will **claim** to lead you closer to God, but if you listen to them, they will take you further away.

So – how do you spot them? What do they look like?

Did you catch the way Jesus described them?

Matthew 7:15
'They come to you in sheep's clothing, but inwardly they are ferocious wolves.'

On the outside they look great! They look like harmless sheep! They look *like anyone else*. Ordinary, everyday people – and when you meet them, you probably instantly like them.

And that's the danger! They don't have a badge on their chest which says: '*Be careful about trusting me*'. They don't have a huge neon sign over their head announcing: '*Danger! False teacher! Bad leader! Stay away!*'

It's easy in the movies. You can always tell who the 'good guys' and the 'bad guys' are. The good guys are likeable, friendly and kind. They drink in moderation and treat their women well. The soundtrack always plays positive, happy music when you focus on them. And the bad guys? They look mean and nasty. They're often dressed in black. They treat people badly. They always have scary or violent music playing whenever they come into the scene.

But in real life, the problem with spotting a false teacher is that '*they come to you in sheep's clothing*'. On the outside, they can look great!

But on the inside? '*They are ferocious wolves*'.

I know of young people who have been torn in two by false leaders. Some have ended up in religious cults where they had to hand all their money over to the group leader. Others have found that the person who asked them to trust him was in fact a sexual predator – simply out for their own enjoyment.

You can meet a false teacher anywhere. Sometimes they are chanting on the street. Sometimes they are knocking on your front door. Sometimes you'll read what they've said in a pamphlet or on a website. Sometimes they can even sneak into your local church.

So – if a false teacher looks so good on the outside, how do you spot them?

3. CHECK OUT THEIR 'FRUIT'

Matthew 7:16-20
'By their fruit you will recognise them. Do people pick grapes from thornbushes, or figs from thistles? Likewise every good tree bears good fruit, but a bad tree bears bad fruit. A good tree cannot bear bad fruit, and a bad tree cannot bear good fruit. Every tree that does not bear good fruit is cut down and thrown into the fire. Thus, by their fruit you will recognise them.'

What does Jesus mean – '*by their fruit you will recognise them*'? What on earth is he talking about?

When I first started as a youth pastor, I moved into a house that had fruit trees everywhere in the backyard! I didn't even know what most of them were!

But there was one tree in the middle of the backyard that took pride of place. And even with my stunted gardening knowledge, I was immediately able to work out that this was an *orange tree!*

Now... how was I able to determine that this particular tree was indeed an orange tree? **Because it had oranges growing on it!**

The fruit on the *outside* of the tree was able to show me what the *inside* of the tree was really like. The orange *fruit* proved to me that *orange life* was running through that tree. And because *orange life* was running through that tree, then I knew I wouldn't find watermelons, or bananas, or pineapples growing from that same tree. It was an orange tree!

In the same way, the *fruit* that people show in their lives is *what is seen on the outside.* It is their character; it is their behaviour; it's what comes through when they're not putting on a pretence.

Here's what Jesus is saying to us: *'Don't be fooled by someone because they have a convincing voice. Don't be fooled by someone because they say nice things about you to make you feel good. Don't be fooled by someone because they're a good preacher. Or because they've got a flashy car or play a mean guitar. **Check out their fruit!'***

'GOD HAS NOT CALLED US TO BE JUDGES, BUT HE HAS CALLED US TO BE FRUIT INSPECTORS'

How do you do that? Simply work out: *'Do they treat others as Jesus would? Do they genuinely care for people? Are they truly forgiving? Do they promote the things of God, or do they only promote themselves? **How do they behave when they think no one's watching?'***

Sometimes you will need the advice of more experienced Christians to help you work that out. You might need to check with your pastor or leader at church if there's something you're not sure about. And you can certainly check with your own Bible to make sure that what you're being taught fits in with what God really says.

We live in a world where some people do the wrong thing. We live in a world where some people will take advantage of you. We live in a world where some people will try to lead you away from God.

Before you give someone your trust, check out whether their life is consistent with someone who loves and obeys Jesus. Then you can avoid **Danger 4 – Listening to the wrong people.**

23 DANGER 5 – FAKING IT

Matthew 7:21-23

1. IT'S SO EASY TO PRETEND

Have you ever 'met someone' online? Met them in a chat room? Written to them on instant messenger? Communicated in an email – but never met them face to face?

What's the difference between meeting someone *online* and meeting them *face to face*?

When you meet them online – you can pretend! You can make up your details – you can pretend to be older, or better looking, or richer, or live in a different country. The other person doesn't know! *(Now I know that **you** would never do this, but does it make sense how **dangerous** it is to form a friendship online? – because you've got **no idea** whether the other person is telling the truth!)*

When the other person can't see you, it's so easy to pretend.

Here's another example:

What's the difference in what guys **say** to their girlfriends, and what they say **about** their girlfriends? That is, when they're standing around with their mates, and they're all talking **about** their girlfriends – what will be different from what they **actually** say when they're with their girlfriends?

They will pretend. They will brag about things that never happened. They will lead their friends on to believe that this girl **really** likes them, when in fact the exact opposite might be true.

When the other person's not around, it's so easy to pretend.

I know that you and I are basically honest people, but let's face it – **we all pretend!**

We pretend to our parents that we have no homework. We pretend to our teachers that we've done our homework. We pretend to our friends that we're more important than we really are. We pretend that we're sick when we don't want to go to school.

We're meant to tidy our room – but we just throw everything in the cupboard and close the door. We pretend that it's tidy.

2. THE DANGER OF PRETENDING

Sometimes it can be incredibly dangerous to pretend.

Imagine that something has gone wrong with the light in the room, and you **pretend** that you know enough about electricity to fix it. So you pull out your screwdriver and start fiddling about with the light switch. If you really don't know anything about electricity, **that would be incredibly risky to do!** Sometimes, pretending can be really dangerous!

Imagine you're pretending that you know stacks about first aid (when really you don't)! You could cause amazing damage!

> I remember when I was doing a first aid exam. The examiner asked a question to the guy next to me – he obviously hadn't done any study, and so he **pretended** to know the answer. The examiner asked him: '*What would you do if a patient had a broken nose?*' His reply? '*Well, if a bone is broken, then you need to attach a splint to keep it straight. So I'd get two empty ball point pens and stick them up his nostrils as splints, and bandage the pens to his face*'.

Hmm. It can be dangerous to pretend!

Or imagine that you have been sent undercover to track down and capture a powerful terrorist. Somebody who has killed thousands of people. You are working undercover – you are trying to work your way into his life – you become one of his trusted advisers while you try to gain his confidence. You are pretending to be his ally, but your real mission is to capture him and take him away for justice.

Can you imagine how dangerous it would be for you to work undercover like this? One false move – and your life is over! It would be incredibly dangerous to pretend when you're dealing with someone who is that powerful.

3. PRETENDING WITH GOD

One of the real traps for living as a disciple is that it's so easy to pretend with God.

You can cry out: *'Lord, I love you with all my heart'*. But deep down in your heart you might not be sure that you love him at all. *'O Lord, I want to obey you'* – but maybe what you really want to do is just keep on sinning.

The **easiest** place to pretend with God is when you're in a Christian group.

You can get really involved at your Christian youth group – looking like you're really getting into worshipping Jesus. But maybe you're really there to pick up the girls. Or you can look really Christian at your Christian school. But maybe you're just doing what your teachers want so things will go well for you. You can be away on a Christian camp – pretending that *'God is working awesome things in my heart'*. But when you go back home – nothing has changed.

'IT'S DANGEROUS TO PRETEND WHEN YOU'RE DEALING WITH SOMEONE POWERFUL'

It's so dangerous to pretend when you're dealing with something powerful. And it's so dangerous to pretend when you're dealing with **someone** powerful.

There is no one more powerful than God. What would it be like if you were to meet up with him now?

4. THE SCARIEST WORDS YOU COULD EVER HEAR

Have a listen to some of the scariest words that Jesus has ever said:

Matthew 7:21-23

'Not everyone who says to me, 'Lord, Lord,' will enter the kingdom of heaven, but only he who does the will of my Father who is in heaven. Many will say to me on that day, 'Lord, Lord, did we not prophesy in your name, and in your name drive out demons and perform many miracles?' Then I will tell them plainly, 'I never knew you. Away from me, you evildoers!''

Imagine the scene. It's judgement day. Jesus has called the whole world around him and every person – living or dead – is standing before him for their final judgement. Jesus is making a decision as to who gets into heaven for eternity, and who misses out.

'IF YOU'VE BEEN PRETENDING WITH GOD – YOU'LL BE FOUND OUT'

There are people crying out 'Lord, Lord...' wanting to be let into heaven. And in verse 21, we read what Jesus will say:

Matthew 7:21

'Not everyone who says to me, 'Lord, Lord,' will enter the kingdom of heaven, but only he who does the will of my Father who is in heaven.'

Jesus is saying: *'Getting into God's kingdom doesn't depend on what you **say**, because if you just **say** something, you can be **pretending**. I'm looking for people who **mean what they say**. I'm looking for people who have done 'the will of my Father''* (And if you're not sure of what this involves, please go back and re-read Chapter 21!).

But people cry out more – and **insist** that Jesus lets them in!

Matthew 7:22

'Many will say to me on that day, 'Lord, Lord, did we not prophesy in your name, and in your name drive out demons and perform many miracles?''

You can imagine the scene. *'Lord – don't you remember what I did? I taught your word to others. I did miracles. I always went to church. I helped little old ladies to cross the street. I said my prayers. I went to my church youth group. I always went on the camps. I joined in at worship. Hey – I was in the band! I became a leader at church. I even bought Christian books and read them.'*

Then Jesus says the scariest words in the Bible:

Matthew 7:23
'I never knew you. Away from me, you evildoers!'

What? Here are all these people – doing wonderful things in the name of Jesus – and he says *'I never knew you. Away from me, you evildoers!'* What's going on?

You see, if you've been pretending with God – you will be found out. If you're just going through the motions – doing the religious stuff, impressing everyone else with how Christian you are – but deep down, you don't really mean it – then Jesus is saying, one day, you're going to be caught out. One day, you will be found out. One day, you'll discover that it wasn't worth it.

Imagine how scary it would be, if on the last day, when you stand before Jesus for your final judgment, he says to you: *'I never knew you. Get away from me, you evildoer!'*

5. THE BEST WORDS YOU COULD EVER HEAR

It doesn't have to be like that. Later in his Gospel, Matthew gives us a **different** response that you might well hear from Jesus:

Matthew 25:23
'Well done, good and faithful servant! ... Come and share your master's happiness!'

Matthew 25:34
'Come, you who are blessed by my Father; take your inheritance, the kingdom prepared for you since the creation of the world.'

There is a grand welcome planned by Jesus for all those who truly belong to him. If you are genuinely following Jesus, you have nothing to fear from meeting him on the last day. Jesus has died to deal with all your sin. Jesus has risen to give you eternal life. There is nothing that can stand in your way of enjoying heaven forever if you are a genuine disciple.

> 'THERE IS NOTHING THAT CAN STAND IN YOUR WAY OF ENJOYING HEAVEN FOREVER IF YOU ARE A GENUINE DISCIPLE'

Jesus' scary words are to warn you of **Danger 5 – Faking it.** And if you think you **might** be just pretending – today is the day to turn back to Jesus and make a decision to be genuine. Decide today to be genuine for eternity.

24 THE CRY OF MY HEART

Matthew 7:24-29

1. A LITTLE LESS CONVERSATION, A LITTLE MORE ACTION

Don't you just hate it when people **say** they will do something, but they never **do** it! Aarrgghh!!

The family version.

'Hey dad – can you come outside and kick the ball with me?'

'Sure son – I'll be out in a few moments.'

You wait outside with your ball, but dad never arrives.

The computer store version.

'We've sent your iPod for repair, and it'll be ready in a week.'

Three weeks later you're still waiting.

The new boyfriend/girlfriend version.

'I'd love to catch up with you. I'll give you a call.'

You wait by the phone. It never rings.

2. IS THERE A PROBLEM WITH YOUR HEARING AID?

Another pet hate of mine – people who never listen!

I went into everyone's favourite hamburger restaurant and I placed my order with the young girl behind the counter. I concluded my transaction by adding: 'And I'd like a strawberry milkshake with that'.

(I had obviously overcome my schoolboy prejudices!)

'Sure' she replied, not even looking up from her computer-cash-register-thingy. 'What flavour would you like?'

I paused for a moment and cleared my throat. 'S-T-R-A-W-B-E-R-R-Y' I said clearly and distinctly so I couldn't possibly be misunderstood.

Fast-forward sixty seconds. She delivers my order to me. Have a wild guess. What flavour milkshake did she give me?

Yep. Chocolate!

Don't you just hate it when people don't take the trouble to listen to you properly?

3. WHAT ABOUT LISTENING TO GOD?

I wonder how God feels when people don't really listen to him? I wonder how God feels when people **say** they will follow him, but don't really do it?

Because right at this stage, you've read most of the 'Sermon on the Mount'.

'WILL I PUT INTO ACTION WHAT I'VE LEARNED?'

You've made it through three chapters of the Bible. You've heard a message from God. If you're going to be a genuine disciple, you need to work out 'What really is 'the cry of my heart'?' Here's the key question: 'Will I put into action what I've learned?'

See if this story sounds familiar:

> ### Matthew 7:24-27
> 'Therefore everyone who hears these words of mine and puts them into practice is like a wise man who built his house on the rock. The rain came down, the streams rose, and the winds blew and beat against that house; yet it did not fall, because it had its foundation on the rock. But everyone who hears these words of mine and does not put them into practice is like a foolish man who built his house on sand. The rain came down, the streams rose, and the winds blew and beat against that house, and it fell with a great crash.'

You've probably heard this story before. It's pretty straightforward. There are two blokes, and they both decide to build a beach house. The first bloke built his house a little further back – on the rocks – where it has a solid foundation. The second bloke wants to get as close to the action as possible – to get the best view – and so he builds his house closer to the surf, right on top of the sand.

Can we pause for a moment? Jesus is pointing out that there is a huge difference between these two house-builders. But before we work out what that difference is, can we first check what that difference is **not**?

Firstly, there's **no real difference between the two houses!** For all we know, they might have used the same architect as each other! They may well have built identical houses!

Secondly, there's **no real difference in how each house is hit by the storm.** Both houses get battered by the same storm! It's not that one is protected, and the other cops it full blast. Both houses get hit by the storm and the wind.

Here is the essential difference: one is built on a solid foundation – and the other isn't. One survives the storm – the other doesn't. But until the storm hits – you can't really pick the difference from the outside. The house-builders know what the difference is – but the casual passer-by probably can't spot it. Until the storm eventually strikes, both houses looked like they were going just fine.

What does the story mean? What's the difference between the two house-builders? Who are they meant to represent? Before we work out what that difference is, can we first check what that difference is **not**?

It's not that one bloke goes to church and the other doesn't. Maybe they **both** go to church! It's not that one hears God's word and the other doesn't. They **both** hear God's word. They both are there at their youth group together. They

'THEY BOTH HEAR WHAT GOD SAYS TO THEM – BUT ONLY ONE OF THEM DOES IT'

both hear the same message preached. They both read the same Christian book.

What's the difference?

Matthew 7:24
'Therefore everyone who hears these words of mine **and puts them into practice** is like a wise man who built his house on the rock.'

Matthew 7:26
'But everyone who hears these words of mine **and does not put them into practice** is like a foolish man who built his house on sand.'

Did you get the difference between the two house-builders? Can you see that their hearts are not the same at all? They both hear what God says to them – **but only one of them does it.**

This happens all the time, doesn't it? You know what God has said on a certain issue, but you simply don't want to do it. You pick the bits about following Jesus that you want to obey. And then you don't really obey him in those bits where it's too hard.

Jesus is describing the difference between a **genuine** disciple and a **counterfeit** disciple. Like the foolish house-builder, the counterfeit disciple **hears** what God says – but can't be bothered **doing** it. And when the storms of God's judgment come on him – his house will not stand.

But the **genuine** disciple not only **hears** what God says, but he **puts it into action.** And on the day when God judges, his house will stand. He will never be destroyed.

If you're going to be a genuine disciple, you've got to work out what sort of 'house' you're building with your life. You've got to work out whether you're just *hearing* God's word, or whether you're committed to *doing* it. You need work out whether you will build your life on Jesus and stand your ground. You've got to work out whether following Jesus is the cry of your **heart**, or just the cry of your **mouth**.

4. IF YOU DON'T STAND FOR SOMETHING YOU'LL FALL FOR ANYTHING

With everyone trying to mould you to become the person that **they** want...with everyone having all sorts of expectations that you feel you've got to live up to... **you must stand your ground!** You've got to make the decisions as to what sort of a man or woman you're going to be. You need to build your life so it doesn't collapse when the pressure is put on.

You've got to live your days so they don't collapse when you stand before God to be judged. And if you build your whole life on Jesus – then you'll never be let down!

When people first heard Jesus preach this message, this was their reaction:

> **Matthew 7:28-29**
> 'When Jesus had finished saying these things, the crowds were amazed at his teaching, because he taught as one who had authority, and not as their teachers of the law.'

I hope that you too are amazed at the fantastic things that Jesus taught. But he doesn't want you to **only** be amazed. He doesn't want you to stand in the crowd and admire him from a distance. Jesus is calling on you to step out from the crowd and follow him. Jesus is calling on you not to just **hear** what he says, but to **put it into action.** Jesus doesn't want you to sit there and just be amazed; he is calling on you to give your whole life to following him. He doesn't just want you as a **maybe** disciple – he wants you to be a **genuine** disciple.

If you have read this book, you have heard God speak to you. You know what he says. You know what he wants. As you read these final words – if you just put the book down and **nothing changes**, then you are building your house on the sand, and one day it will all collapse.

But if you have a genuine heart to follow Jesus – if you're gearing your life up for **genuine success** – if you're determined to give Jesus **genuine obedience** – if you're surrendering to Jesus in **genuine worship** – if you're willing to offer God **genuine trust** – and you're being careful to avoid the **genuine dangers** – then by the power of God's Spirit, you will be enabled to live as a **genuine disciple!**

5. SO – WHAT'S THE CRY OF YOUR HEART?

God wants you to live for him. And he wants you to be genuine. The **pretend** disciple is someone who **says** they're following Jesus but can't be bothered *doing* it. If you want to be a **genuine** disciple – and to remain genuine throughout your life – then make a decision **every day** that you will live **that day** for Jesus. And if you're **living** it – and not just **talking** about it, then like that wise house-builder whose house did not fall because it had its foundation on the rock, then **you will not fall** because your life has its foundations on Jesus – the rock!

That's genuine success – that's genuine obedience – that's being a genuine disciple.

Is that the cry of your heart?

Acknowledgements

Thanks heaps to...

Jesus Christ. Without you, not only would there be no book, but I would have no life. You have taken me to The Father, and filled me with your Spirit. Without you, I can do nothing.

my wife, Karen. Without you, I could not do this ministry. I deeply appreciate the way you put up with me as I wrote each page. You've made lots of helpful comments and timely corrections to what I have written. I love you!

my daughter Carly, and my son Joshua. The youth ministry 'out there' means nothing to me compared with the joy of bringing you two through to Christian adulthood. Thanks for putting up with me as your dad.

some very special students who helped me finish this book:

A number of students from Crossfire took the time to read through my manuscript — and came back to me with all sorts of helpful suggestions. This book is so much better because of you! So thank you to:

Nicole Allison, Emma Barnett, Patrick Bertoldo, Ashleigh Best, Nicola Bracewell, Rebekah Collins, Ben Darwall, Jason Darwall, Thea Furnass, Ashleigh Gibson, Craig Given, Ben Gray, Jessica Greene, Anna Hempstead, Jessica Hickson, Kaitlyn Jones, Rebekah Kent, Leanne Khoo, Robert Kneen, Adrian Lee, Eleanor Lewis, Katherine McCarthy, Hannah Montgomery, Claudia Nicholls, Jacinta Ong, Anita Paratore, Sam Perryman, Tim Price, Caronwen Richards, Rachel Scoular, Paris Shepherd, Ben Simmonds, Tim Simmonds, Emma Simpson, Ilze Simpson, Emma Squires, Monica Sullivan and Melanie Wilson,

the many gifted Bible teachers who have sown into my life over the decades:
I have been blessed over the years by being taught God's word faithfully by a myriad of people — many of you would barely know that I exist. Thank you for what you have taught me. This book is a result of your faithfulness.

the students and leaders at 'Crossfire' in sunny downtown Castle Hill. Thank you for allowing me to take you on the exciting journey of having your life turned around by Jesus. I love hanging out with you guys and I know God will use you to impact this world.

I have taken great care to give due credit to those who have impacted my life and ministry. After almost three decades in ministry, it is possible that I have inadvertently included material which has not been properly acknowledged. If this has happened, please contact the publisher so that this can be rectified in future editions.